A History & Guide
· TO THE ·
Monuments
of Shiloh
NATIONAL PARK

STACY W. REAVES

To Sue,
Best wishes
Stacy W. Reaves

To my dear friend,
Best Wishes
Janie Beal

Charleston H London

THE
History
PRESS

Published by The History Press
Charleston, SC 29403
www.historypress.net

Copyright © 2012 by Stacy W. Reaves
All rights reserved

First published 2012

Manufactured in the United States

ISBN 978.1.60949.412.4

Library of Congress Cataloging-in-Publication Data

Reaves, Stacy W.
A history and guide to the monuments of Shiloh National Park / Stacy W.
Reaves.
p. cm.
Includes bibliographical references.
ISBN 978-1-60949-412-4
1. Shiloh National Military Park (Tenn. and Miss.)--History. 2. Shiloh National
Military Park (Tenn. and Miss.)--Guidebooks. 3. Monuments--Shiloh National
Military Park (Tenn. and Miss.)--Guidebooks. 4. War memorials--Shiloh National
Military Park (Tenn. and Miss.)--Guidebooks. I. Title.
E473.54.R33 2012
976.2'975--dc23
2011046697

Select Monuments

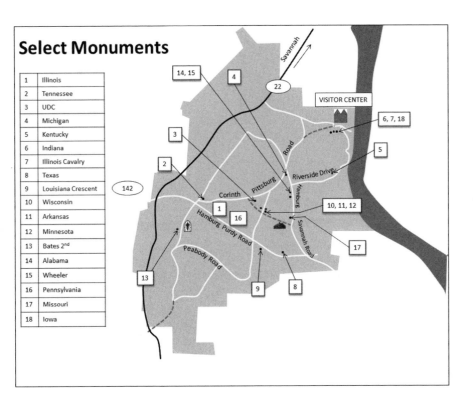

1	Illinois
2	Tennessee
3	UDC
4	Michigan
5	Kentucky
6	Indiana
7	Illinois Cavalry
8	Texas
9	Louisiana Crescent
10	Wisconsin
11	Arkansas
12	Minnesota
13	Bates 2nd
14	Alabama
15	Wheeler
16	Pennsylvania
17	Missouri
18	Iowa

CONTENTS

Preface   7
Acknowledgements   11

1. The Battle of Shiloh   15
2. A Land with Ruins—Creating a Military Park   31
3. Union Monuments   39
4. Confederate Monuments   89

Epilogue   123
Bibliography   125
About the Author   128

PREFACE

O ver the past three years, I have been working with a ninety-year-old retired U.S. Army Air Corps/Air Force colonel. The colonel has spent the past twelve years collecting military artifacts related to World War II and other wars involving Oklahoma soldiers. The collection now has over two thousand artifacts ranging from his hand-dyed air force overcoat to dog tags belonging to a female nurse in the Korean War and a full uniform of an Oklahoma Forty-fifth Infantry soldier in Iraq. The colonel has displayed the collection in various places, but for the past three years he has been trying to establish a museum. It is his goal to make sure that future generations do not forget his fellow soldiers and to teach others of their sacrifice. He has a personal stake in wanting to preserve the story of those who served in wars. The colonel himself served as a glider pilot in Europe during World War II and later as a radio operator and pilot in the U.S. Air Force. He eventually retired in the 1960s.

While working with the colonel, one feels and senses his urgency. Most of the men he served with in the Second World War have passed on, and the colonel wants to see these men honored and to make sure others do not forget their deeds. With every meeting, he reminds me that he may not have long and that time is of the essence. While researching the monuments of the Shiloh National

Military Park, one can hear that same sense of urgency in the voices of the Civil War veterans of long ago. By the early twentieth century, their ranks were thinning, memories were fading and the veterans felt a need to memorialize those who were lost on the battlefield and to educate future generations about their deeds.

For most of the Shiloh veterans, this battle was a defining moment in their lives—one they would never forget. The majority of the soldiers who fought in the battle had never before experienced combat. They were raw recruits. Many had only enlisted in the military a few short months before the battle. For Union soldiers, the encampment at Pittsburg Landing was supposed to be a time for building up the army and training the new recruits. Instead, it became the largest and most fierce battle of the western theater. Before their eyes, they witnessed friends, relatives and even their enemies wounded and killed in a most horrific manner. Over the two days of fighting, 23,746 men would be killed, wounded or simply reported missing.

Despite the end of the fighting, the horror continued. Union soldiers remained on the battlefield after the battle. Their ghastly job was to inter the dead. The bodies, quickly decomposing and badly mangled, made the task formidable. They interred their comrades in large trenches with others from their unit or in individual shallow graves. Union soldiers interred their enemies' bodies in large trenches or hastily dug shallow graves. Some simply rolled the bodies into ravines and threw dirt over them.

In 1866, the Federal government created a National Cemetery at Pittsburg Landing for the proper and honorable burial of the Union dead at Shiloh and from other sites along the Tennessee River. The Confederate bodies remained interred on the battlefield. Local farmers returned to their land after the battle and continued to plow fields and grow crops. Often, the hastily buried bodies of the soldiers were unearthed during farming operations. More than thirty years after the battle, human remains continued to be unearthed.

Veterans of the battle began visiting the battlefield to view the sites and remember where they were "baptized" into war. Despite the area sustaining little physical change since April 1862, the veterans felt the need to have the battle site preserved. They believed this would prevent graves from being disturbed in the future and allow others to study and develop an understanding of the great battle. More importantly, it would allow them to honor those who served. By the 1890s, the once young soldiers were aging and dying. During the late nineteenth and early twentieth centuries, the white-haired soldiers worked tirelessly to erect monuments and memorials on the newly preserved battlefield park of Shiloh.

Today, granite soldiers gaze through the dim smoke of a long-ago battle; some stand at parade rest while beautiful women in long flowing gowns climb steps, protect the nation or tend to the wounded. Each year, thousands of visitors from all over the world wander the fields reading the tablets and gazing at the monuments. Often, they stop to snap a photo and to pose in front of the monuments representing their home states. Few know of the efforts and dedication required to fund, create and erect each monument. Though visitors admire these works of art, few know the symbolism that each represents or the story that the veterans were trying to convey to future generations. Much like the retired colonel in 2011, it was the hope and dream of the Shiloh veterans that people would not forget their courage, deeds and sacrifices of long ago in 1862. It is my goal to see that the veterans' work is continued. This book is an effort to educate battlefield visitors about the monuments' symbolism and the work of the veterans to create a memorial to their deeds and sacrifices.

ACKNOWLEDGEMENTS

S omeone once said that it takes a village to raise a child. What most people do not realize is that it takes a village to write a book. I experienced the enthusiasm, support, assistance and guidance of many people, without whom this project would never have come to fruition. However, please realize that their help does not mean that they are responsible for the final product. All the mistakes, oversights and just plain stupidity are mine.

The ability to conduct the research and locate obscure sources would not have been possible without the wonderful staff at Tulsa Community College. Evelyn Rogers and her staff in the interlibrary loan department have searched for books and articles and even tolerated my requests for them several times in a row. Mary Estrada and her staff at the southeast campus library deserve special mention. They have been helpful in finding sources and putting rushes on requests. In addition, chats with Mary were always encouraging and kept me going throughout the project.

Of course, I cannot overlook the numerous archives, libraries and museums that have given me access to their collections. I owe a big debt of gratitude to Ashley Berry and Heather Smedley at the Shiloh National Military Park. They endured some very cold days in the collection's building, as well as assisting me with scans, finding material and in general acting interested in my finds. Sharon Grimes of the Richard W. Bock Museum at Greenville College and Mary Lou Eichorn at the New Orleans Historical Society cheerfully opened their collections and helped find materials. I also owe a debt of gratitude to the archivists and librarians at numerous facilities for copying records and checking collections; these include the Historical Society of Iowa, the Illinois State Historical Society, the Indiana Historical Society, the Pond Spring Historic Site, the Wisconsin Historical Society and the Tennessee State Library and Archives.

Several people who simply love the history of Shiloh contributed a great deal to this project. They provided interviews, photos and research material or simply pointed me in the right direction. I am thankful to Mrs. Bettye Stanley for sharing her United Daughters of the Confederacy (UDC) history, files and stories. Her love and dedication to the Tennessee Monument is remarkable. I would also like to thank Jon Ross and the Hardin County Historical Society for their assistance with photos. I owe a special debt of gratitude to Brian K. McCutchen. He made this project easy by paving the way with his master's thesis and then generously assisting me by finding photos from his own research.

I wish I could take credit for the wonderful contemporary photos of the monuments. Alas, I do not have the photography skills. I cannot thank Jimmy and Linda Christopher and Jane Beal enough for taking time from their schedules to create the beautiful photos. They have captured the absolute beauty of the monuments. I hope that park visitors will be inspired to linger longer and study the art of the monuments.

I have to give special mention to someone who took on a boring and mundane task: Janie Lampi. I cannot repay her enough for volunteering to proofread and help edit this manuscript. I appreciate her eagle eye and comments. I am still not sure if she is truly excited to read this or just trying to cure insomnia.

And finally, I owe the following people more than I can even express. While many people do not get along with their mothers-in-law, I can truly say that I have the best. My mother-in-law, Alice Reaves, has been a great motivator and a source of encouragement and support. I thank my grandparents and parents for always supporting me, babysitting the kids and taking an interest in my work. The people I can never repay are my husband, George Reaves IV, and our three daughters—Bessie, Camille and Claire. They have endured many weeks of Mommy in her office writing, taking research trips and going on numerous visits to the park. In their own way, they have encouraged me. My husband has blessed me in so many ways. He is the one who told me to go for it, provided the babysitting, funded research trips and did countless loads of laundry and cared for our children while I wrote. His love and support are more than I can ever hope to repay.

1

THE BATTLE OF SHILOH

God grant that I may never be the partaker in such scenes again...When
released from this I shall ever be an advocate of peace.
—*Soldier after the Battle of Shiloh*

Years after the Civil War, Union general and former U.S. president Ulysses S. Grant wrote, "Shiloh was the severest battle fought in the West during the war, and but few in the East equaled it for hard, determined fighting." Shiloh was indeed one of the fiercest battles in the western theater of the war. It quickly proved to the Federals that they should not underestimate the Confederates. The Confederate army went into battle believing it could defend the western portion of the Confederacy and that General Albert Sydney Johnston would lead it to independence. The Rebels returned from the battle defeated and without their beloved general. Legend has it that after the Battle of Shiloh the South never smiled again.

Pittsburg Landing and Shiloh Church were not critical points in the Confederate or Union war strategies, but the battle would be significant. Early in the war, the Union army had developed a strategy that called for taking the Mississippi River Valley in the West and dividing the Confederacy. In February 1862, General Grant and flag officer Andrew H. Foote moved southward into northern Tennessee and quickly captured Forts Henry and Donelson.

Because of these victories, Rebel general Albert Sydney Johnston, commanding the Army of the Mississippi, retreated from Kentucky and middle Tennessee to the town of Corinth, Mississippi. The town was a key city for the Confederacy. It contained a railroad junction for the Memphis & Charleston and the Mobile & Ohio Railroads. The Charleston & Memphis was the only direct east–west railroad in the South. Johnston began to mass his army in the sleepy town in hopes of holding the Mississippi Valley and protecting the vital railways.

In March 1862, following its successes at Donelson and Henry, the Union army began preparing to advance farther south in hopes of gaining further regional control. Major General Henry Halleck ordered Union troops to the river town of Savannah, Tennessee. Union plans called for General Don Carlos Buell's troops to march overland from Nashville and join Grant's troops along the Tennessee River. From there, the army could strike the Confederates in Corinth and seize the railroad. Grant moved his troops from Savannah to Pittsburg Landing, approximately nine miles upstream. Believing the Confederates were preparing to defend Corinth, General Grant focused his attention on training and drilling his men. The largest majority of his men had never seen combat and lacked formal military training. After Buell arrived, the Union army planned to attack the Confederates.

The Confederates, trying to recover from losing Kentucky and middle Tennessee, were not waiting for the Union troops to come to them. General Johnston, under political pressure to regain territory, began formulating an attack on Grant's army. On April 2, Johnston received word that Grant was waiting for Buell's troops to join him. The Confederate general realized that the time to strike the Federal troops was now. He developed a plan to attack Grant's troops at Pittsburg Landing before Buell arrived. The attack, actually prepared by General Pierre Gustave Toutant Beauregard, his second in command, called for turning the Union army's left flank and cutting it off from the river. This would force Union troops into Owl Creek and surrender. With approximately forty-five thousand soldiers, Johnston began moving his army north into Tennessee. He hoped to attack Grant's unsuspecting army by April 4. Muddy roads, poor terrain and green soldiers slowed the Confederate advance. With so much delay and contact made between the Rebel scouts and Union troops, General Beauregard feared that the element of surprise was lost. Determined to regain the lost ground and show Confederate strength, Johnston continued with his orders of attack. However, he moved the date to the morning of April 6.

As the sun slowly rose over the Tennessee River that morning, the day appeared to be like all the other Sundays in camp with nothing out of the ordinary. The Union soldiers began stirring from their night's slumber. They calmly got dressed and began brewing coffee. However, this morning would not remain peaceful for long, and the day would be one not soon forgotten by either side. Confederate troops began advancing through the woods and fields. As they approached the Union soldiers' camps, the Rebels began firing. The unprepared Yankee soldiers scrambled to get their weapons, form lines of defense and hold off their Confederate attackers. The Battle of Shiloh had begun.

The Confederates had nothing to fear—they had not lost the element of surprise. General Grant had not bothered to prepare defenses at Pittsburg Landing. Confident there would be no attack, the Federal commanders had dismissed reports of Rebel activity around the area just days before. The Fifty-third Ohio Infantry's commander, Colonel Jesse Appler, had spotted Confederate cavalry near his camp on the evening of April 4. Fearful of an attack, Appler began to prepare his men. The colonel sent a courier to inform Union general William T. Sherman of the approaching enemy. An irritated Sherman sent the messenger back, telling the colonel to take his regiment back to Ohio and claiming that "there is no enemy closer than Corinth." Colonel Everett Peabody, a Federal brigade commander whose troops were camped near the front position, had heard and seen enemy activity for three days prior to the battle. Believing that the troops were not prepared for a possible attack, Peabody sent out a patrol late on the evening of April 5. His men came back and reported potential enemy activity and even the sounds of the Confederates in front of their camps. Fearful that an attack was imminent, Peabody sent out a patrol just before dawn on the morning of April 6. About 4:55 a.m., the patrol neared Seay's farm, where it encountered fire from Rebel cavalry. A line formed to hold off the enemy. However, after an hour of fighting, the Union soldiers retreated.

It quickly became apparent to the Union soldiers that this was not a small group of skirmishers. This was a full-scale attack. Colonel Jesse Appler, aroused from his sleep with reports of firing, formed a line in front of his camp and sent word to General Sherman that the enemy was at hand. Sherman, having heard this type of report from Appler earlier, did not respond favorably. Reportedly, the general replied, "You must be badly scared over there." Despite the sarcastic remark, Sherman did decide to investigate. As he neared the camp of the Fifty-third Ohio, he saw the rising sun glistening off Rebel bayonets. He realized that the Ohio colonel was not exaggerating and reportedly exclaimed, "My God, we are attacked!" The Union troops began falling back through their camps. As the Confederates followed, many stopped in the camps to partake of the abandoned breakfasts and supplies left behind.

Confederate commanders Johnston, William Hardee and Braxton Bragg worked to keep their army organized and moving forward. By 9:00 a.m., the Confederates began full assaults on the scrambling Yankee troops. Johnston ordered divisions to attack Sherman's troops around Shiloh Church. By 10:00 a.m., troops were charging Sherman's men. Sherman had already taken heavy losses and had lost three guns. As a result, he ordered his men to fall back. Federal general Stephen Hurlbut had begun moving his troops forward to the front from his camps near Cloud Field. By 9:00 a.m., he had positioned his 4,400 men along Widow Sarah Bell's cotton field to the right of the Hamburg–Purdy road and waited for the enemy to come. As other Union commands fell back or moved forward, they positioned themselves along an old farm road that ran from Duncan Field to an old peach orchard and Sarah Bell's cotton field. On the far right, Federal troops also formed along the Locust Grove Branch. By 10:00 a.m., General Benjamin Prentiss's troops, some of the earliest camps overrun by the enemy, had joined the line, adding 1,200 men. This put the total number of men along the half-mile farm road (later called the Sunken Road) at approximately 6,200 strong, with twenty-five cannons supporting the infantry. The sound of cannon fire told General Grant that his assumptions about the Confederates were wrong. That morning, as Grant ate breakfast in his headquarters at the home of William Cherry in Savannah, he had heard the sounds of firing in the distance. He set down his coffee, headed for his headquarters' boat *Tigress* and began moving toward Pittsburg Landing. As Grant boarded the boat, he sent orders to Buell to take his men to the riverbank opposite Pittsburg Landing instead of meeting in Savannah. Upon arrival, the general found his men under fire and the landing a scene of chaos and confusion. Men, terrified, fled from the front and took refuge at the river, where the fighting had not yet reached. The Union commander quickly realized that this was a full-scale attack on his army and that he needed immediate reinforcements. Grant sent orders for General Lew Wallace to march his troops overland from Crump's landing, four miles upstream. To reach the battle, Wallace needed to march his seven thousand men along the Hamburg–Savannah road and cross the bridge at Snake Creek. This would put him in the rear of the Union right—Sherman's troops. Due to a lack of clear knowledge of the local area, Wallace and his men would not arrive on the battlefield until late in the evening of April 6. He would be too late to offer much assistance to Grant's men that day.

As the Union troops formed a strong defensive line, the Confederates regrouped. Shortly after 11:00 a.m., General Beauregard ordered attacks on the Federal center along the old Sunken Road. About noon, Confederate general Braxton Bragg took command of the center with a determination to break the line and force the Yankees to retreat. He ordered the Louisiana and Arkansas brigades under the command of Colonel Randall Gibson to attack. The Union fighters repelled the attack, and Gibson sent word back to Bragg that he needed artillery support. The colonel regrouped his men and made a second attack on the Union center. Federal troops, in an effort to repulse the Confederates, opened fire with artillery from Captain Andrew Hickenlooper's Fifth Ohio Battery. Again, Gibson retreated. Dense underbrush and heavy firing from the Union troops, who were under cover from the slight indention of the road and the underbrush, made the charge on the Yankee line almost impossible. The Confederate lines broke up, and some of the men in the rear accidentally fired on the men in the front. Colonel Henry W. Allen of the Fourth Louisiana, wounded through both cheeks, explained to General Bragg that they needed more support. Bragg, unfazed by Allen's condition and determined to break the Union line, ordered Gibson's brigade to charge the Yankee position. Again, the Confederates met intense firing. This time they took cover, fired at their enemy until they ran out of ammunition and retreated.

The fighting along the center became so intense that soldiers would remember it for the rest of their lives. The intense barrage of shot and shell that the Confederates encountered reminded many of a "hornet's nest." Years later, this would become one of the names for the fighting along the old wagon road. The Confederates threw 18,000 men against the Union center. However, the Rebels employed piecemeal assaults, using no more than 3,700 men at a time. The results were tragic. Southern soldiers fell to the ground, dying in the most unforgettable manner. One Union soldier was appalled to see that bodies did not just litter the ground but that the dead and wounded lay in piles. Many were headless, cut in half and disemboweled. This was a sight that soldiers on both sides would never forget, and it would motivate them to preserve the battlefield and give recognition to their deeds and sacrifices.

Disorganization among the Confederates gave the Union left under Generals Sherman and John A. McClernand an opportunity to regroup and make a strong offensive. A pause in the fighting occurred about noon when the Confederates took a moment to regroup and rest. They had been fighting since dawn, and many were tired and hungry. The overrun Union camps provided the soldiers with food and other items for personal use or as trophies. Federal commanders took advantage of this pause. Having already lost their camps and been forced back to Jones Field, Sherman and McClernand counterattacked. Their assault was successful. The Confederates fell back half a mile. This allowed the Yankees to recapture McClernand's headquarters. North of Wolf Field, the Union attackers halted and regrouped in the wood line. The Rebels, not anticipating that Federal forces would counterattack,

The Battle of Pittsburg Landing. German lithograph from the late nineteenth century depicting fighting during the Battle of Shiloh. *Photo CN3097, used with permission from the Tennessee State Library and Archives.*

hastily scrambled to reorganize and build their line. Once the Confederates regrouped, they threw their forces into stopping the Union advance, and by 2:00 p.m., they had regained the advantage. The Union troops retreated once again to Jones Field. Realizing that they did not have enough power to hold the field, they fell back to Tilghman Branch.

As the Northern troops in the center and left fought to hold off the Confederates, the right was holding a strong defensive line. Having settled along an old cotton field, General Stephen Hurlbut readied his men for the oncoming Rebel attacks. At noon, General Johnston deployed General John Breckinridge's reserve troops against the Yankees along Sarah Bell's cotton field. The Union line held. About 1:30 p.m., Johnston received word from Breckinridge that Colonel William Statham's Forty-fifth Tennessee refused to attack again. One of Johnston's aides and Tennessee governor Isham G. Harris went to rally the Tennesseans. They returned unsuccessful. Johnston decided to go and motivate the frightened soldiers to advance. Upon finding the unit, the general took a tin cup that he had taken from a Union camp earlier and tapped the bayonets of the soldiers as he rode along their line. Johnston told the men, "These must do the work. Men they are stubborn, we're going to have to use the bayonet." Upon reaching the center of the line, he yelled, "Follow me!" Turning on his horse, Johnston led the troops forward. He stopped and watched the troops make the attack. Governor Harris returned from delivering an order to find Johnston in the southeast corner of the peach orchard. He immediately noticed that the general did not look well and asked Johnston if he was hurt. He replied in the affirmative and said that he feared it was serious. As Johnston began reeling in the saddle, the governor led his horse down a ravine. With the assistance of the general's aide, Harris lowered the commander to the ground and began searching for the wound. He soon found it in the hollow of the knee. The bullet had severed the main artery, and the general was quickly bleeding to death. Unfortunately, his staff physician was out on the battlefield tending to the wounded, as directed by Johnston. Within minutes, the Confederate general had taken his last breath on the battlefield.

For years after the battle, many argued that when General Johnston died, the South lost the battle. After Beauregard received word of Johnston's death about 3:00 p.m., he continued the fight. The general began shifting forces from his right to the left, where the sounds of heavy fighting were occurring. Many of the troops fighting Sherman and McClernand began shifting toward the southeast as well. This left but a small number of Confederates opposing Sherman's troops in the late afternoon. The Rebels were focusing their attention on the hornet's nest. Under pressure from the Confederate attacks, the Union troops north of the peach orchard began to turn. Hurlbut's line made a ninety-degree angle to Prentiss and Wallace along the Sunken Road. By 4:00 p.m., Hurlbut had retreated up the Hamburg–Savannah road. Eventually, McClernand's troops on the Union right retreated, too. This left the Rebels focused on the Union center. Beauregard sent General Daniel Ruggles to locate and assemble all the cannons he could find.

In all, the Confederates were able to amass parts of eleven batteries, or roughly sixty cannons. Within four to five hundred yards of the Federal front, the Rebels let loose a barrage of artillery fire. This was the largest concentration of artillery in North America up to that time. The Union line, bowing under the pressure, began to cave in and form a horseshoe shape. The Confederates continued to attack from the east, north and south. About 5:30 p.m., the Rebels surrounded the Yankee troops in the hornet's nest, thus forcing General Prentiss to surrender 2,250 Union troops.

Grant, unwilling to give up, prepared to make one final stand and hold out until Buell and Wallace arrived. The Union soldiers prepared to defend Pittsburg Landing and save their army. Late in the afternoon, as units retreated to the landing, Grant began forming a final defensive line near the river. Federal colonel Joseph Webster placed guns into a line and coaxed the stragglers back into battle. Rebel officers ordered their men to pursue the retreating Union troops. However, this was more difficult than expected. Many of the Confederates were running out of ammunition, the Union gunboats had opened fire upon them and, as they neared the Tennessee River, they discovered the ravines filled with water and the hills very steep. Little did the Rebels know as they pushed to take the Federal army that reinforcements were arriving at Pittsburg Landing to aid Grant. By late afternoon, parts of Buell's army had arrived and were being ferried across the river. As the troops stepped onto the landing, officers directed them into position. Confederates moved through the ravines to attack Grant's last line of defense. Sometime after 6:00 p.m., as the sun began to set, Beauregard realized that his men were exhausted and that night was quickly approaching. The general called off the Southerners' attacks for the night. Tired, hungry and disorganized, the Rebel army failed to form a line and instead wandered back into the Northern camps looking for food and a place to rest.

Despite the intense fighting the day before and the horrors of the battlefield during the night, the battle continued on April 7. Grant, reinforced by Buell and Wallace, now had approximately forty-five thousand troops ready to fight. He began shelling the Confederates at 6:00 a.m. This time the Union army caught the Southern troops off guard. Their men were intermingled among various regiments and scattered across the battlefield. During the night, many had simply deserted. Some of the troops had retired as far away as four miles from the landing. Beauregard scrambled to organize his men and to defend the ground he had gained the day before. By 10:00 a.m., the Confederate commander was finally able to put together a line of defense of approximately twenty-eight thousand men and eighty cannons. The Northern troops began attacking their enemy over the same ground they had lost the day before. Fighting among the wounded and dead, the Confederates made several weak counterattacks. Despite their attempts to hold their ground, the Rebels were no match for the stronger Union troops. By 2:00 p.m., Beauregard realized that he had no reinforcements coming to aid him, and he could not hold out any longer. The general called for a retreat. Despite having fresh troops, Grant did not follow the fleeing Southerners back to Corinth. His men were exhausted.

Although the fighting was over, the battle was not completely finished. Immediately, Grant's army began cleaning up the battlefield. The Union soldiers were to remain on the battlefield to finish preparing for a future offensive. Grant removed the bodies to prevent the spread of disease and to show respect for the soldiers. The Union soldiers took great care in burying their own men but hastily buried their enemy in trenches, ravines or shallow graves. The stench and the decomposing bodies made the work unbearable. Ultimately, the remains of the battle would take years to remove.

The Battle of Shiloh was only the beginning of the hard-fought battles with astonishing loss of life. The Confederates reported that they lost 10,699 men. The Union army reported 1,728 dead, 8,012 wounded and 959 missing. Grant alone reported that his army had 1,513 dead, 6,601 wounded and 2,330 missing or captured. General Buell, who saw action late in the battle, reported losing only 241 men to death, 1,807 wounded and 55 missing. In total, the Federals sustained 13,047 casualties from the battle. For the soldiers who fought the battle, these were friends, family and fellow soldiers. The shock and horrors of the battle were very real. Years later, survivors would visit the battlefield to remember those hours of sheer terror they had survived and to memorialize their bravery and the loss of comrades.

The loss of life, the reality of war and the desire to keep Americans from forgetting and thus repeating such bloodshed are what motivated veterans of the Civil War to preserve the battlefield. Shiloh held a special place in the memories and hearts of the veterans. Reports circulated that the farmers living on the battlefield were inadvertently disturbing the graves of the soldiers. In 1866, deplorable burial conditions motivated Congress to establish a national cemetery at Pittsburg Landing. This allowed the remains of the Union soldiers to receive proper burial and grave markers. Because they were considered traitors, the Confederates remained buried on the battlefield. Despite this attempt to provide decent burial, local farmers, wagon traffic, road crews and livestock continued to unearth soldiers' remains. Individual graves were being lost to fires, erosion and local farming. Rumor had it that local hogs that ran wild often uprooted bodies. Bones of the soldiers littered the fields and woods. These conditions and stories deeply bothered a group of Army of the Tennessee veterans who visited the battlefield in 1893.

As this group of Union veterans left the battlefield on board the steamer *W.P. Nesbit*, they discussed how to preserve the battlefield. Already, a group of Antietam and Chickamauga veterans had successfully petitioned Congress to preserve their battlefields as national parks. The Shiloh group believed this would be the best way to protect the remains of their fellow combatants, to honor the veterans of the Army of the Tennessee and to preserve the site of the battle. The veterans created the Shiloh Battlefield Association and held their first formal organizational meeting in Indianapolis, Indiana, in 1893.

The creation of the Shiloh Battlefield Association allowed veterans of both sides to organize their efforts at creating a national park. At their first meeting in 1893, the organization outlined three major goals. The first goal was to ask the government to purchase the battlefield. The second goal was to preserve all graves, including Southern graves, on the battlefield. Finally, the association wanted to appoint a special committee whose task was to get the support of the various veteran organizations in lobbying Congress. Along with outlining goals, the association elected officers to oversee the organization. The first president of the group was none other than former Union major general John A. McClernand. McClernand had commanded a division of the Army of the Tennessee at the Battle of Shiloh. Other officers included E.T. Lee, who had served as a private with the Forty-first Illinois Infantry at the battle, and Dr. J.W. Coleman, a surgeon of the Forty-first Illinois. The association made former Union generals Benjamin Prentiss, Lew Wallace and Don Carlos Buell honorary vice-presidents. Each of these men had led troops during the battle. General Lew Wallace held some prominence in post–Civil War society. He had recently served as the governor of New Mexico Territory and had just finished publishing the great novel *Ben-Hur*. Wallace's support of the project would help garner additional supporters in the political realm and among veteran organizations.

After thirty years, bad feelings between the North and South had begun to wane, and the Union veterans sought to preserve the site not just for their benefit but also for that of their former enemies. To garner support of Southerners, the association asked former Confederate generals Basil Duke and Joseph Wheeler to serve as officers. It also appointed former Tennessee governor and current Democratic senator Isham G. Harris to the board. All three men had served at the Battle of Shiloh, and two would play a role in marking the battlefield. Senator Harris had served as an aide to Confederate general Albert Sydney Johnston and had been with the commander when he died during the battle.

In order to achieve its ultimate goal, the Shiloh Battlefield Association had to solicit support of congressional members. Congressman David B. Henderson was the perfect candidate to help get legislation passed. Henderson had served with the Twelfth Iowa Infantry during the Civil War and first saw combat at Fort Donelson and later at Shiloh. Henderson also had a brother killed and buried on the battlefield. Henderson himself received a wound to the leg during the battle for Corinth, Mississippi. After surgeons removed his leg and the army discharged him from service, he later reenlisted in the Forty-sixth Iowa. After the war, Henderson pursued a career as a lawyer and became a congressional representative in 1883. While serving in Congress, the representative gained power and influence by serving as the Judiciary Committee chair and as Speaker of the House. Henderson would have great weight and influence in passing legislation for a military park.

Meanwhile, the Shiloh Battlefield Association began recruiting membership and soliciting donations. The association began advertising its creation and goals in the various veterans' magazines and newspapers. Along with making its presence and objective known, it requested donations toward its cause. Its work was successful; by 1895, the group boasted twelve thousand members. To gain and retain membership, members were required to pay dues, and in return, the association planned reunions on the anniversary of the battle and continued working toward legislation for the preservation of the battlefield. By 1895, the organization had accumulated enough support and donations that it was able to purchase 2,600 acres of the battlefield. The idea was to transfer the land to the federal government once Congress had the money to establish the park.

Meanwhile, in Congress, Henderson worked diligently to garner support and pass a bill to preserve the battlefield as requested by the aging veterans. Gettysburg had already become a memorial park; however, it favored the Union army. The Shiloh veterans wanted to show reconciliation and honor both armies that had fought the war. Veterans of the Chickamauga battle had preserved the site and created a military park. This is what the Shiloh veterans hoped to create. Henderson and the Army of the Tennessee veterans decided to follow the successful formula established by the Chickamauga group. The best way to follow their example was to enlist the aid of their primary leader, General Henry Boynton. The former general had served at the Battle of Chickamauga and, years after the war, visited the site with a fellow veteran. Moved by the atmosphere of the battlefield and their intense memories of the battle, the two men successfully lobbied Congress and established the Chickamauga National Military Park in 1890. This would be the first of the federally operated national military parks. Boynton helped Henderson draft the bill establishing Shiloh as a national military park and served as an advisor to the Shiloh veterans.

With many Civil War veterans serving in Congress, along with the influence of Henderson, it was not difficult to get legislation passed. Boynton and the congressman created a bill with eight sections. In the first section, the two men proposed that the government purchase the land from private owners and that the State of Tennessee cede land to the federal government for the park as well. In the bill, they envisioned the park encompassing three thousand acres. The purpose for the creation of a battlefield park at Shiloh was to honor the armies of the Southwest. Section two of the bill addressed the oversight of the battlefield. The War Department would have jurisdiction over the park's administration. The secretary of war would have ultimate say over the site and could acquire land through condemnation.

Much of the battlefield belonged to farmers. Some had owned the land prior to the war. Section three addressed the issue of residents on the battlefield. The government allowed these residents to lease the land. The rental agreement allowed the families to remain on their land and to work their fields for subsistence. However, these tenants had to agree to preserve the historical integrity of the park, which would also include future monuments.

Lastly, Henderson and Boynton added a fourth provision that specified the creation and oversight of the park by a three-man commission. This commission would report to the secretary of war but had oversight of day-to-day operations. The bill stipulated that the commission must consist of three veterans of the battle. More specifically, it must have one representative for each of the three armies engaged in the battle; this included one Confederate veteran from the Army of the Mississippi. More than likely, Boynton suggested this arrangement. The Chickamauga National Military Park maintained this same organization. On June 22, 1894, representative Joseph H. Outhwaite submitted bill HR 6499 to the House for approval. It met with enthusiastic support. The Committee on Military Affairs added a stipulation to the bill that the land be marked before the veterans passed away. The committee declared, "It would be a monument to them before they left this world."

On December 27, 1894, President Grover Cleveland signed the act creating the Shiloh National Military Park. Now the task was to appoint members of the commission that would oversee park operations. Henderson began petitioning Secretary of War Daniel

Lamont to appoint veterans Cornelius Cadle and David W. Reed to the commission. Reed had served with the Twelfth Iowa Infantry during the battle. On the first day of fighting in the hornet's nest, he received a wound to his thigh and remained on the battlefield throughout the night unable to surrender or move. The next day, as the battle raged on, Union troops retook the land and Reed. The army sent Reed north to Illinois for medical treatment, and upon his recovery, Reed returned to the warfront. By war's end, he had obtained the rank of captain. Of all the battles Reed fought, Shiloh had the most impact and remained a lifelong interest. Lamont made him the park commission's secretary and the park historian. Reed's great fascination with the battle would serve him well. It was his task to locate and document the troop positions and movements during the battle and to write its first official history.

The commission still lacked a chair. With much support from Henderson and others, Cornelius Cadle received the appointment. He would represent the Army of the Tennessee, and like Reed, Cadle was an Iowa veteran of Shiloh. He had served as an adjutant with Colonel Abraham Hare of the Eleventh Iowa Infantry. After being wounded during the Vicksburg campaign, the army mustered him out. Cadle later rejoined the army and ended the war with the rank of brevet colonel. Later, he became a businessman with interests in coal mining. Cadle's business sense made him a great candidate to oversee the commission.

Secretary Lamont appointed retired general Don Carlos Buell to represent the Army of the Ohio. Buell had led the Army of the Ohio at the battle and provided the men needed to help Grant finish the fight. Despite what appeared to be a promising military career at Shiloh, Buell lost his command after failing to pursue the Confederates after the Battle of Perryville in late 1862. After a hearing, Buell resigned from the army in 1864. He pursued a quiet life working with a coal mining company in Kentucky and as a government pension agent. Despite his lack of political influence, Buell would be involved in making sure the positions and movements of his army were correct in history and on the battlefield.

The commission required a representative from the Confederate Army of the Mississippi. The secretary of war bestowed the honor on Colonel Robert F. Looney. Prior to the war, Looney had been a prominent lawyer in Memphis. When the war broke out, he supported his home state and raised the Thirty-eighth Tennessee Infantry. He commanded this unit at the Battle of Shiloh and throughout the war. Afterward, the stately Southerner resettled in Memphis, Tennessee, and invested in large amounts of land in Memphis and Mexico. Although not a politician, Looney was well respected among Tennesseans and acted as a liaison between the state and the commission.

With the commissioners appointed, it was time to begin constructing the Shiloh National Military Park. To start the work, they needed an engineer. Atwell Thompson, who had worked on the Chickamauga battlefield, took the position. It was his responsibility to survey the land and begin building roads. The commission also hired Savannah, Tennessee lawyer Captain James W. Irwin to act as a land agent in the purchasing of the land. Everyone was in place to create a battlefield park and memorial. David Reed would study the history, find the locations and movements of the armies and mark them on the battlefield. Atwell Thompson would survey the land, build the roads and assist veterans in erecting monuments. Captain Irwin would clear the titles and purchase the land. Now, the veterans could begin telling their story.

2

A LAND WITH RUINS—
CREATING A MILITARY PARK

A land without ruins is a land without memories—
a land without memories is a land without history.
—*"A Land without Ruins," by Abram Joseph Ryan*

After the Battle of Shiloh, residents returned to their farms to find them ruined and their land littered with the debris of war. Spent bullets, ramrods, torn canteens and haversacks littered the old farm road that Union soldiers had defended so valiantly on April 6. The peach trees in the orchard near Sarah Bell's old cotton field had the blossoms ripped from their limbs by bullets. There would be no peach crop that summer. Residents began cleaning up and attempting to return to normal life. By the time the battle's veterans started coming back to the former battlefield, the farmers had cleared woods for new fields and let some fields return to forest, and some roads were no longer in use. The land around Shiloh Church and Pittsburg Landing was slowly changing over time, and so was America.

The late nineteenth century was a period of rapid change and growth in America. The country was becoming more industrialized, and capitalism began to rule. Factories were getting bigger, and businesses were becoming more organized. Corporations, in the modern sense, emerged. The barons of industry, such as Andrew

Carnegie, became very wealthy. The cities of America grew larger and were crowded with new immigrants from Southern and Eastern Europe. New inventions were improving the lives of Americans. The country was advancing and moving forward. The old soldiers feared that as America changed, their battlefields would disappear and the nation would forget their heroism. Just a few short years after the war ended, veterans began organizing societies that reunited them with their former comrades. The first veterans' organization, the Third Army Corps Union, began holding reunions as early as May 1865. Within three years after the war, both the Army of the Ohio and the Army of the Tennessee organized veterans' societies. These groups met often in reunions and hosted presentations about the various battles in which the men had fought.

It was common for the veterans to visit their former battlefields as part of a reunion or on personal visits. Both Gettysburg and Chickamauga had become destinations for veterans and curious tourists. Americans visited the fields wanting to see famous sites of battle. Lincoln's address and the prominence of the Gettysburg

Buggies and carriages parked in the hornet's nest, circa 1900. This could have been from a dedication ceremony or a veterans' reunion. *Photo courtesy of the Shiloh National Military Park.*

battle made the site popular with tourists and veterans alike. Locals set up identifying markers for famous locations, and some gave tours of the battlefields. As people became interested in the war, the veterans grew concerned that Americans would not have the correct information. They worried that their heroism would be overlooked or, even worse, incorrectly recorded. The old soldiers feared that the battlefields and their sacrifices would lose meaning. The sites would become nothing more than scenic parks for picnics and afternoon strolls. This spurred the drive to preserve the battlefields and accurately mark the battle lines. The veterans, hands shaking and eyesight beginning to fail, spent their spare time comparing battle reports, writing memoirs and recording the history of their units. Magazines and veterans' societies published these accounts, and the former soldiers debated the significance and accuracy of each account. However, as time passed, not only did the land change, but so did the graying soldiers' memories. To make matters worse, their ranks were beginning to thin. The veterans believed

Reunion of the Confederate Tennessee Second Infantry. *Photo 12062-SU 173, used with permission from the Tennessee State Library and Archives.*

Pittsburg Landing, circa 1900. *Photo 8223-HD026, used with permission from the Tennessee State Library and Archives.*

that future generations would not have an accurate story or a clear understanding of the war. To the aging men, it became imperative to preserve the battlefields and to be accurate.

The remoteness of the Shiloh battlefield precluded it from becoming a tourist destination after the war. To visit the site, one had to travel by wagon on country roads or by steamboat. During the 1880s, veterans began traveling to rural Hardin County wanting to revisit the Shiloh battlefield. Life had continued here, and residents gave little thought to the great battle that had occurred just a few years earlier. Preservation of the battlefield and returning it to its 1862 appearance became the largest task facing the commission.

As park historian and commission secretary, David Reed became responsible for accurately compiling the battle history and locating battle lines. The land still had battle scars. Trees with bullet holes stood as silent markers of the battle, but the forest had reclaimed some fields, and some wooded areas were gone. Reed set up a residence in a tent at Pittsburg Landing and began oversight of daily park operations. Like the other battlefield parks, Shiloh was to have every troop position marked with a tablet. The markers would record the units, times and battle actions. Reed began poring over the recently published *Official Records of the War of Rebellion.* This was a compilation of both Confederate and Union officer reports from the entire war. These records allowed the park historian to follow the after-action reports and locate the battle lines. To further aid Reed's research, visiting old soldiers accompanied him in a black buggy across the battlefield identifying their troops' actions of long ago. After Reed and the commission were satisfied that the battle lines were accurately established, they erected iron tablets. By simply following the tablets, a visitor could follow a troop's movement from the beginning of the battle to the end. In all, 651 tablets dotted the battlefield guiding visitors through the events of April 6 and 7, 1862.

The commission left nothing about the armies' positions and movements unmarked. Using iron markers shaped to look like the front of a sidewall tent, it marked all the Union troops' campsites. Reed and the commissioners decided to mark the headquarters of brigades and divisions and the death sites of generals differently from camp and troop positions. Atwell Thompson had been a

The headquarters monument marking the headquarters of General William T. Sherman. *Photo courtesy of the Shiloh National Military Park.*

road engineer at the Chickamauga battlefield park. Drawing on his experiences there, he suggested using condemned cannon shells to create an elaborate marker for the generals' headquarters. Thompson created a four-sided pyramid of artillery shells for these monuments. The final design of the headquarter monuments called for concrete bases and eight eight-inch shells along the bottom row of each side. Approximately 134 artillery shells completed each pyramid.

Five commanders—General Albert Sydney Johnston, Colonel Julius Raith, Brigadier General Adley H. Gladden, Colonel Everett Peabody and Brigadier General William H.L. Wallace—lost their lives during the battle. A monument marked where each received his mortal wound. To differentiate the mortuary monuments from the headquarters monuments, the commission came up with a different design. The mortuary monuments would be rectangular with concrete bases. The very center would have a twenty-four-pound Parrott siege gun positioned vertically. Four smaller pyramids would decorate the four corners of the base.

By 1899, the park commission and the War Department had established guidelines for monuments and memorials erected by

Mortuary monument for General Everett Peabody. *Photo courtesy of Shiloh National Military Park.*

states and other interested groups. They wanted memorials that would withstand time, visitation and weather. They also wanted monuments that would need little maintenance. One of the first requirements for any monument erected in the park was that it be made of granite, bronze, marble or a combination of these materials. Those wishing to erect a monument submitted the proposed design, dimensions, weights, inscriptions and materials to the park commission. The secretary of war gave the final review and approval of the proposal.

Park historian David Reed would become a key player in the erection of monuments in the park. Concern for accuracy extended to the location of monuments. Scenic view or proximity to the tour route would not play a role in their placement. Regulations governing the monuments placed regimental monuments on brigade lines closest to where the regiments had engaged in notable fighting. Regiments that were detached or had become separated from their own brigades and had distinguished themselves during the battle could place a monument near the site of their contributions. States with troops engaged in the battle could erect a general state monument on the grounds. Often, state commissions relied on historian Reed's judgment and accuracy in locating the best position for their monuments.

Regulations concerning the memorials required that all inscriptions be purely historical and factual. They could not praise individuals or groups, nor could they censure any person or action. All inscriptions could relate only to the Battle of Shiloh and conform to the official reports. Although a few groups found it disappointing that they could not praise the heroic actions of their leaders and men or point out the faults of a leader, they complied without argument. Reed and the park commissioners had to approve all inscriptions before they went to the secretary of war for final approval. At times, Reed's study and understanding of the battle did not agree with that of members of a commission or regiment. After reviewing the inscriptions for the Fifteenth and Sixteenth Iowa monuments, the park historian rejected them, causing an argument between the park commission and the Iowa commission over the accuracy of the events recorded on the proposed monuments. After three years, the secretary of war made a final decision on these inscriptions.

3

UNION MONUMENTS

The late nineteenth and early twentieth centuries became an era of monuments. Prior to the Civil War, monuments in public spaces had been few, and most were erected to military commanders or national leaders. The post–Civil War era changed the landscape. The interest and push by Civil War veterans to tell their story created a surge in monument construction. The need to honor those who served and those who did not return spawned a drive in small-town communities to erect memorials. Veterans pushed not only to preserve the battlefields but also to erect memorials to honor the common soldier and to provide a lasting record of his deeds.

A monument industry quickly developed to meet the rising demand. At the turn of the twentieth century, monument companies flourished. Catalogues and magazines published by the United Daughters of the Confederacy and veterans' organizations all carried advertisements. Readily available stock monuments allowed organizations that were unable to obtain a professional sculptor to erect memorials inexpensively. The granite statue of the watchful soldier at parade rest or at attention became popular due to advertising, pricing and availability. Many companies kept sculptors and stonecutters in their employ. The increase in demand led the Hughes Granite and Marble Company of Ohio to employ fifty-five master stonecutters, sculptors and engineers.

The push for memorializing and preserving Civil War battlefields coincided with a renaissance in American art and architecture. Inspired by the celebration of American industrialism and history at the Philadelphia exposition in 1876, artists and architects began creating buildings and sculptures in a neoclassical style. Their work celebrated American nationalism, idealism and nature. In 1877, just a year after the Philadelphia exposition closed, the Society of American Artists and the Society of Decorative Arts formed. These two organizations were at the forefront of this rebirth in American art, sculpture and architecture.

The Chicago Columbian Exposition of 1893 further sparked this new trend in American architecture and sculpture. Daniel H. Burnham, the exposition's director of works, wanted something to make the fair memorable and stand out from those of the past. The 1889 Paris Universal Exposition had made a splash with the Eiffel Tower. Burnham needed something to rival it. He decided that the architecture of the entire fair was its crowning glory and began hiring the most talented young artists and architects the country offered. This included Frederick Law Olmsted, who had previously designed Central Park in New York City, and John Morris Hunt, who had designed the pedestal of the recently dedicated Statue of Liberty. These men, along with countless others, designed the hundreds of white plaster buildings and sculptures that graced the grounds.

The fair's art and architecture reflected and promoted the Beaux-Arts style. By the mid-nineteenth century, American artists and writers had begun moving to Paris to study art. At the time, the École des Beaux-Arts in Paris usurped Rome and Florence in prominence for art training. As a result, the school influenced an entire generation of American artists. Those who were not fortunate enough to study in France trained under master sculptors who had. In 1882, America boasted thirty-nine art schools, fourteen university art schools and fifteen different decorative societies. Artists spent time studying the human body as art, much as the Renaissance masters had done centuries before. As a result, much of the artwork favored the human form, and most compositions were allegorical in nature. Many of the newly created art institutions and societies often held expositions allowing the artists to display their art, thus allowing the public to see their creations and talent, as well as advertise their services. The renaissance in American art provided veteran groups and others with a large number of sculptors to hire. The Beaux-Arts style lent itself to the form the veterans desired and created monuments that aptly told the story of the war, the sacrifices of the soldiers and the gratefulness of a nation. Because the American Renaissance and the push for memorials intersected at the same period in history, many of the Civil War monuments found at Shiloh and other battlefields reflect this artistic style.

Illinois Monument

There were none more brave than you, Illinois.
—Omitted quote from the Illinois monument

Although the state of Illinois was not the first to erect a monument to its soldiers on the Shiloh battlefield, it put great effort into perpetuating the memory of its soldiers. The state had good reason to be interested in erecting monuments on the battlefield. It was one of the most represented states in the battle. Illinois soldiers made up five divisions of the Army of the Tennessee. Illinois commanders led four of those five divisions. The state of Illinois sacrificed 3,957 of its sons during the two days of fighting, including Major General William H.L. Wallace.

The soldiers of Illinois participated in the battle's fiercest fighting. Major General Benjamin Prentiss's Sixth Division first encountered the enemy and eventually surrendered 2,200 men in the hornet's nest. Four regiments of Illinois troops made up Colonel Julius Raith's brigade. Those four regiments sustained heavy losses during the early fighting at Shiloh Church on April 6. General McClernand fought to hold the area around Shiloh Church and keep the route open for Lew Wallace's troops later in the day. Hurlbut's men fought to the line in the peach orchard. Perhaps the biggest loss was that of Major General William H.L. Wallace. Wallace's men had moved

Illinois State Monument, by Richard W. Bock. *Photo by Jimmy and Linda Christopher.*

up to help create a defensive position along the old farm road, later known as the Sunken Road. As the Confederates began to encircle the hard-fighting Yankees, Wallace began withdrawing his men from the fighting about 5:00 p.m. As Wallace took his foot from a stirrup to dismount, a bullet struck him in the head. He fell facedown. An orderly tried to carry his body to the rear but was unsuccessful. The man moved the wounded commander only a mile before he had to give up. He lay Wallace out of the way of oncoming soldiers. The Confederates did not recognize the wounded general or notice that he was still alive. Legend has it that sometime in the night a Confederate soldier gave the dying commander a drink of water.

Unbeknownst to General Wallace, his wife, Ann Wallace, was at the battle that fateful day. She had taken a boat to Pittsburg Landing to surprise her husband. Ann arrived at the landing just before daybreak aboard the *Minnehaha* and sent word to her husband of her arrival. It was not until the wounded started arriving at the river that the general's wife realized a battle was raging. Word reached Ann that her husband was engaged in battle and could not come to her aboard the steamer. She remained aboard and tried to comfort the wounded and assist the medical staff the best she could. Late in the day, a chaplain with the Twentieth Illinois returned to the boat and informed the loving wife that her husband had been hit in the head and was lying on the battlefield. Throughout the night, the worried and grieving Ann nursed the wounded and tried not to think about her beloved husband dying on ground now held by the enemy. The next morning, at about ten o'clock, word came to her that some men had recovered her husband and that he was still alive. The soldiers brought Wallace's body to the boat, and Ann rushed to his side. The general, unconscious, lingered for four days until he finally died at the Cherry House in Savannah, Tennessee.

Illinois veterans were quick to respond to the call for assistance in marking the Shiloh battlefield. In 1897, the state senate authorized a ten-person commission to mark the positions on the battlefield. Former general John A. McClernand chaired the commission. The lean, white-bearded general, along with the other commissioners, reviewed battle reports from the Illinois units and toured the battlefield with historian David Reed,

The Illinois Shiloh Commission visiting the Shiloh battlefield, circa 1902. *Photo courtesy of the Shiloh National Military Park.*

locating positions. Despite changes to the area, the commission was able to find the circular marks of the Sibley tents used in the camps and other signs of the battle.

To perpetuate the memory of its brave sons, the Illinois legislature passed another bill. In June 1899, the state provided funding for the erection of monuments on the battlefield. Initially, the state appropriated $65,000 for monuments for each regiment and one monument for each battery. In addition to these, the state specified the erection of one monument to represent the entire state not exceeding $10,000. The state authorized the commission to create a memorial to the late general William H.L. Wallace. After learning that the federal government had built the monument to Wallace, the state added another $10,000 to the funding for the state monument, thus bringing the total funds for the state monument to $20,000.

After receiving several bids for the regimental monuments, the committee selected the Culver Construction Company of Springfield, Illinois. The company did not have an elaborate design, but it bid $470 for each monument. It would be the company's responsibility to create the monuments, engrave them, transport them and set them on the battlefield. The regimental monuments were to give information about each regiment during the battle and honor them with individual recognition.

Chairman McClernand and the commissioners envisioned the state monument as an elaborate memorial that would convey a sense of Illinois' sacrifice and heroism. In 1899, the commissioners put together a design competition offering a $250 award. "These competitions are avid morsels for so-called granite monument dealers. In this particular competition, twenty-seven designs were submitted, including mine and that of one legitimate architect," recalled sculptor Richard W. Bock. The state commission reports record only eleven different artists and companies submitting designs. However, all agreed that Bock's design was the best. The artist noted that at a meeting in Springfield on January 3, 1900, "after everyone had had his say about the merits of his own design, the architect...got up and spoke in laudable terms with reference to my design, saying that there was nothing in any other designs present worthy of consideration. The final result was that I was given the first prize."

Richard W. Bock's design was simple but impressive. The sculptor submitted a large drawing of a huge granite shaft slightly tapering at the top. An American flag was draped over the top of the shaft "as though carelessly laid there." An American eagle with his talons grasping the shaft overlooked the entire scene. On the front of the column, Bock had included a bronze panel with a bold relief depicting a battle scene.

For the thirty-six-year-old artist, this was his largest and most challenging commission. The Chicago sculptor, born in Germany in July 1865, immigrated to the United States with his family at the age of five. During his teen years, Bock studied drawing at the Mechanics Institute of Chicago. In 1885, convinced that he had learned all he could about sculpture in Chicago, he headed to New York, where he quickly secured a job with Allen and Ketson. Bock worked with the company on the Vanderbilt House on Fifth Avenue. This would be his first taste of carving and sculpting for a home. Bock left New York to enroll in the Berlin Academy in Germany,

STATE OF ILLINOIS

TO COMMEMORATE THE SONS WHO ???
GAVE THEIR LIVES TO PERPETUATE
WITH HONOR AND HER GLORY, ????

Sketch of the original proposed monument for the state of Illinois, by Richard W. Bock. *Photo courtesy of the Richard W. Bock Museum, Greenville College, Greenville, Illinois; Sharon W. Grimes, director.*

where he spent a year studying art. In 1890, wishing to round out his studies, the sculptor went to Paris to study at the famed École des Beaux-Arts in Paris. After three years of study in Europe, Bock returned to the United States ready to work. In 1891, the city of Chicago was preparing for one of the biggest events in its history: the Columbian Exposition. Bock managed to secure a commission creating sculptures for the Mining and Metallurgy Building and the Electricity Building. With this job, he joined the ranks of other great upcoming artists who created short-lived masterpieces for the fair.

In 1893, a group of veterans in Lancaster, Pennsylvania, solicited designs for a monument dedicated to the Pennsylvania soldiers on the newly created Chickamauga battlefield. Bock's design of two soldiers defending the flag won. On November 13, 1897, the veterans of Pennsylvania dedicated the monument. During this time, Bock made the acquaintance of a young Chicago architect named Frank Lloyd Wright. Wright would use Bock's designs for his innovative architecture. In 1896, the architect commissioned the artist to create a plaster relief for the Isidore Heller House in Chicago. This was the beginning of a long working relationship between Wright and Bock. From 1891 to 1903, Bock would complete six public commissions, as well as numerous architectural sculptures, for Frank Lloyd Wright and many other noted architects.

The Illinois monument at Shiloh would be one of Bock's most challenging projects, both in size and demand. Looking back, he recalled that the contract with the State of Illinois "proved to be a very interesting experience." A few days after winning, the commission held a meeting with the artist. Although it really liked Bock's design, it wanted a change. The group decided that it wanted a

Preliminary sketch by Richard W. Bock of the revised Illinois state monument. *Photo courtesy of the Richard W. Bock Museum, Greenville College, Greenville, Illinois; Sharon W. Grimes, director.*

statue on top of the shaft. Many communities around the country were erecting shaft monuments with a statue of a solider on top. It is unclear if this is what the committee had in mind. No matter, Bock used his creative genius to design a statue that would convey the feelings and emotions of the Illinois soldiers.

Veering away from the standard soldier at parade rest, the sculptor created a statue in the Beaux-Arts style. Bock considered his new design to be quite simple. This time, it included a statue of a woman "representing the mother of Illinois, holding a sheathed sword on her lap. Her other hand held a book upright upon the block on which she was seated. It represented the illustrious history of Illinois and her honored sons who had played such an important part in preserving the Union." To begin work, Bock needed to create a working model of a woman. The artist turned to his beautiful wife, Martha, for his model. She had recently given birth to their first child, Dorathai, and she was busy tending to the needs of a newborn. Bock decided that the best thing to do was to make a plaster cast of her entire figure.

Martha Bock posing at her husband Richard W. Bock's studio in Chicago. *Photo courtesy of the Richard W. Bock Museum, Greenville College, Greenville, Illinois; Sharon W. Grimes, director.*

> *The whole performance took no more than two hours' time and gave me a permanent model from which I could make my one-quarter-size nude working study. When that was done, I dressed up my life cast with the drapery I desired and then did the same with the model.*

After Bock had completed the model of the mother of Illinois, the Shiloh committee visited his studio to approve it. Upon securing the committee's approval, the sculptor created a full-size model for casting the bronze figure. Bock made the eighteen-foot model in plaster rather than clay. He believed that the "rugged surface of the plaster would be entirely in keeping with the nature of the subject—more than the smooth surface of modeled clay." After completion, the bronze foundry owner visited the studio to decide how to dismember the model for transportation to its facilities for casting.

The front of Bock's plaster model of the mother of Illinois. *Photo courtesy of the Richard W. Bock Museum, Greenville College, Greenville, Illinois; Sharon W. Grimes, director.*

The back of the plaster model of the mother of Illinois sitting in the artist's Chicago studio. *Photo courtesy of the Richard W. Bock Museum, Greenville College, Greenville, Illinois; Sharon W. Grimes, director.*

Bronze relief of the battle scene on the pedestal of the Illinois Monument. *Photo by Jane Beal.*

Bock turned his attention to the inscriptions and the battle scene relief. This time, he used his friends and neighbors as models. The artist believed that without using models, "realism would have been unobtainable by using a purely imaginary variation of the faces." An eighteen-year-old boy by the last name of Liebchen joined Bock's group of friends in modeling the soldiers' faces. During the First World War, the young man became a well-known film star by the name of Stewart Holmes. To make sure the small sculptures had perfect body posture, Bock modeled the figures nude first and then added the uniforms. Beneath the relief panel, the artist included part of the Gettysburg Address: "The world will little know nor long remember what we say here, but it can never forget what they did here."

As Bock finished the state monument, the Illinois commission began placing the regimental monuments on the battlefield. Although these were considerably smaller than the state monument, it was still

Oxen haul an Illinois regimental monument across the park. *Photo courtesy of the Shiloh National Military Park.*

a major undertaking. Everything going to Pittsburg Landing arrived by steamer, as there were no direct rail lines. Once at the landing, a crane hoisted the monuments off the boat. The steep road leading up from the river presented a challenge in hauling the heavy stones. The park engineer working with the monument contractor set up a block and tackle along the landing to pull the monuments up to the top. Once at the top of the road, oxen carried them down the cleared and graveled roads of the park. Atwell Thompson, the park engineer, created a large frame scaffolding structure at the base of the Illinois Monument. Using a small engine, the construction crew hoisted the large stones into place and eventually lifted the lower half of the statue to the top; then, the head and shoulders were lifted and attached.

The commissioners decided to create a special monument to the Illinois cavalry. They turned once again to Richard Bock. This time, the artist's style moved toward a design that was more geometric and a rejection of the Beaux-Arts tradition. Much like the linear, geometric designs created for Wright, Bock created a pentagon-shaped monument. He likened it to a hitching post. On each side of the pentagon, he posted bronze panels that commemorated the Illinois regiments.

On May 17 and 18, 1904, the State of Illinois dedicated its monuments. Park commission chair Cornelius Cadle accepted the

The Illinois Cavalry Monument, by Richard W. Bock. The monument is designed to represent a hitching post. *Photo by Jane Beal.*

Artist Richard W. Bock stands in front of the plaster model of the Illinois State Monument in his Chicago studio. *Photo courtesy of the Richard W. Bock Museum, Greenville College, Greenville, Illinois; Sharon W. Grimes, director.*

monument on behalf of the United States government. Former Confederate general Basil Duke, a member of the park commission, gave the oratory speech to mark the occasion. Although Bock did not attend the ceremonies, he believed that he could "claim without exaggeration that [he had] made a definite contribution to art."

Indiana

I have been made a scapegoat.
—*General Lew Wallace's address at the dedication of Indiana monuments*

Indiana had the third largest number of troops participating in the Battle of Shiloh. Nineteen infantry regiments, two artillery batteries and one cavalry regiment took part in the bloody battle. These Indiana men served in some of the most intense fighting of the battle. Troops under General Stephen Hurlbut fiercely defended the hornet's nest along the center of the Union line on April 6. The Forty-fourth Indiana Infantry, commanded by Colonel Hugh B. Reed, repulsed four of Confederate colonel Randall Gibson's assaults on the hornet's nest. So intense were the shot and shell that the woods surrounding them caught fire. By the time the regiment withdrew to support the siege guns near the landing, seven color-bearers had sacrificed their lives while holding high the Union flag.

Another large number of Indiana soldiers arrived late on the battlefield on April 6 to provide assistance and reinforcements to General Grant's men. General Lew Wallace, a native of Indiana, camped with 7,000 men at Crump's Landing some four miles down the river from Pittsburg Landing. After the battle began, General Grant called for Wallace to come quickly with his men. What happened with Wallace has been a source of controversy and confusion. Some reports claim that the orders from Grant were verbal and that Wallace would not accept unwritten orders. All seem to agree with Wallace's reports that he became confused over which road to take and had to rely on local guides to find his way. Nonetheless, he arrived late in the day on April 6. His troops, which

The Indiana Second Cavalry Monument. *Photo by Jimmy and Linda Christopher.*

had several Indiana regiments, provided fresh reinforcements for the defense of the landing and the renewed fight on April 7. The state of Indiana lost 1,250 of its sons on those two bloody days in April.

Thirty-nine years after the battle, the governor of Indiana appointed a commission to oversee marking battle positions and the erection of monuments. Six veterans of the battle were part of the seven-person commission. Members of the committee visited the battlefield to locate battle lines. General Lew Wallace himself visited for three days. Reed and the general traced the route from Crump's Landing to Shiloh. They backtracked and turned around numerous times as the general became confused and disoriented. A local who had been living in the vicinity on that fateful day in April and was still residing there stopped to help the general get his bearings.

After agreeing on battle positions, the committee sent out circulars asking for designs and bids for regimental monuments. Approximately 150 different monument makers, foundries and artists submitted entries. The committee selected the design by John R. Lowe. Besides liking the design, the committee liked the artist because he was a native of Indiana. Lowe, born in 1842, had served with the Eleventh Indiana under Major General Lew Wallace at the Battle of Shiloh. Near the end of the war, Lowe found himself in Baltimore with his regiment. Due to his location, Lowe had the distinct honor of serving as a guard over Abraham Lincoln's body after the president's assassination in 1865. After the war, the artist returned to Indiana, where he worked for the Wetmore and Morse Granite Company of Indianapolis. Lowe created the design, and the Muldoon Granite Company in Louisville, Kentucky, rendered it in granite.

The state legislature of Indiana appropriated $25,000 for the erection of nineteen infantry and two artillery battery monuments. Lowe created twenty-one monoliths, each with a raised design of crossed sabers for cavalry and crossed rifles for infantry and further decorated with military accoutrements. The seal of the State of Indiana graced the top of each monument. Because each regiment and battery received its own monument, the back sides included inscriptions about the units and their actions during the battle.

Although these were not as large as the state monuments of Illinois or Iowa, it was not a simple task to transport and erect the heavy

The relief carvings on the Indiana Fifty-first Infantry Monument. *Photo by Jane Beal.*

stones. Each had a base of eight feet, two inches square; a height of sixteen feet, six inches; and a weight of twenty-seven thousand pounds. The size and weight would not be the ultimate problem in placing the monuments on the battlefield. The first shipment of the monuments arrived in August 1902. As the Muldoon Company lifted one of the granite bases, it slipped and broke apart. Using wagons and oxen, the men hauled the heavy stones across the battlefield. The company's wagon wheels were less than six inches wide, and they tore up the park roads. Cadle put a halt to all transportation of the stones until they found wagons with larger wheels. As it happened, the Illinois commission was placing its monuments on the battlefield at the same time, and it allowed Muldoon's men to borrow its wagons. This was a minor problem quickly overcome. The weather and the Tennessee River were bigger challenges. As the monument company placed the three monuments and few bases that had arrived on the battlefield, it waited on eleven cars carrying the rest of the memorials. The summer heat had lowered the level of the river, and the barges, only drawing four feet of water, were stopped along the river unable to continue until the river rose another three feet. Two weeks later, park commissioner James Ashcroft reported to Chairman Cadle that "the Tennessee is drying up; hence, there is no prospect of moving stone soon." At the end of September, Ashcroft happily reported that heavy rains had finally raised the river enough for the barges to move again.

Due to the delays in shipping and erecting the monuments, the Indiana commission delayed its dedication ceremonies until spring. It chose to unveil and dedicate the monuments on the forty-first anniversary of the battle and became the second state to hold such ceremonies. Former general Lew Wallace chaired the event, and Indiana governor Winfield T. Durbin presented the monuments to the government. As chair, Lew Wallace addressed the gathered crowd of veterans and families. He took the opportunity to explain what had happened with his troops at the battle and told the crowd that he had become the "scapegoat of the battle." Richard W. Bock, the artist of the Illinois Monument, happened to be at the park that day and took a few moments to attend the Indiana ceremonies. He commented on the general's remarks:

> *Therefore, he again brought censure upon himself from the press for his improper conduct, and so, alas for the General, he was once again in chancery. In his speech he might have said, "With all due respect for the immortal, the world will little note nor longer remember what I say here; but I have tried to do my best."*

On his way home, Bock saw the general at the train station in Indianapolis. He noted that Wallace spent his time walking up and down the hall. To the artist, the aged commander seemed "like a lost soul…for I knew what was troubling him, and there was no help that anyone could offer."

Iowa

Now don't you believe you have kept the American eagle captive long enough?
—*Sculptor Frederick Triebel to E.B. Soper, chairman of the Illinois commission*

As the frail, elderly men stood gathered around a monument surrounded by woods, they could not help but feel both pride and

The Iowa Monument, by Frederick Triebel. *Photo by Jimmy and Linda Christopher.*

sorrow. The men were the survivors of the Iowa Hornet's Nest Brigade. They had gathered on the Shiloh battlefield in observance of the battle's fiftieth anniversary. Years earlier, many had gathered around the same monuments in order to dedicate them; now they gathered to reminisce and take pride in the monuments they had erected. These men had been part of Prentiss's brigade, which held off the determined Confederate attacks along the hornet's nest on April 6. A large portion of these men had surrendered to the enemy late that evening and spent months in Confederate prisons. Those who did not surrender moved back to Pittsburg Landing, forming one last line of defense. The men of Iowa had helped Grant defend Pittsburg Landing and then followed him to Corinth and Vicksburg.

The state of Iowa had sacrificed a large number of its sons to the brutal war. It was no surprise that in 1894, the Iowa General Assembly responded to the requests of the Civil War veterans to pay tribute to them. An eleven-man commission took on the task of locating the battle positions on the Chattanooga battlefield. A year later, the legislature appointed a commission for the Shiloh battlefield. By 1900, the Iowans had located all their battle lines at Shiloh, and the state legislature appropriated $50,000 for state and regimental monuments.

Determined to find the most fitting design and the best location for a monument, the committee visited the battlefield and toured the sites defended by Iowans years ago. After selecting a location, they returned to Iowa and put out a circular calling for designs for both state and regimental monuments. After some consideration, the committee selected a design by New York sculptor Frederick Triebel and a standard design offered by Shenan and Flavin for the regimental monuments.

By the time the Iowa commission had selected Frederick Triebel's design, he was an accomplished sculptor. Triebel, the son of a stone carver, grew up in Peoria, Illinois. Aspiring to be more than a stone carver like his father and brothers, the sixteen-year-old moved to New York to study sculpting. After a short time in New York, he moved to Boston to study art, and in 1880, he moved to Florence, Italy. After finishing his studies, Triebel moved back to the United States and

The Iowa Monument, built circa 1906. *Photo by Jane Beal.*

began looking for commissions. Like many other artists of the time, he found himself drawn to the Columbian Exposition in Chicago. There, he served as a juror for the International Sculpture Exhibition. In 1894, Triebel moved back to Florence, Italy, to teach as a fellow of the Royal Academy of St. Luke.

In 1902, Triebel submitted his design to the Iowa Shiloh Monument Commission. Understanding that the committee wanted to honor and perpetuate the memory of the Iowa soldiers in the battle, he created a large monument with allegorical figures. A seventy-five-foot column of granite made the center of the monument. A bronze eagle mounted on a bronze globe crowned the top of the column. On one side, a bronze figure of a woman ascended the steps with a pen in hand. The woman, known as Fame or the Muse of History, inscribed the deeds of the Iowans on the pages of history. On the opposite side, Triebel placed a bronze laurel wreath framing a scroll.

The design submitted to the Iowa commission was not an original one by Triebel. The sculptor had used the same design for a Civil

Above: The Italian bronze eagle and globe represent the Illinois soldiers defending their country. The eagle's wings span sixteen feet. *Photo courtesy of Shiloh National Military Park.*

Right: The bronze figure of Fame, also called the Muse of History, climbs the steps of the Iowa Monument to inscribe the deeds of the Iowa soldiers at Shiloh on the pages of history. Her bare breast represents all the mothers left childless because of the battle. *Photo by Jimmy and Linda Christopher.*

On the Iowa Monument, opposite of Fame, there is a laurel wreath covering a scroll recording the battle. *Photo by Jimmy and Linda Christopher.*

The face of Fame, by Frederick Triebel. *Photo by author.*

War monument in Peoria, Illinois, but with a variation. The Peoria monument included two large bronze statues of battle scenes on the front and back. It seems that Triebel submitted the Peoria design with different inscriptions and with only Fame and the eagle and globe. The new design, although somewhat taller, was simpler. Perhaps he reworked the design so that it would be less busy and to make a bolder statement. The Peoria monument cost considerably more money than the Shiloh one. Perhaps he simplified the design to reduce the cost. By using the same design, he could reuse the molds of Fame and the eagle and globe.

Triebel had a personal connection to the monument's sculptures. His beautiful young wife modeled for the figure of Fame. Santina, an orphan adopted by two maiden women, modeled at the art school in Florence where Triebel studied. They met in a studio where the young Italian woman was sitting for a class Triebel was taking to learn to sculpt hands. He immortalized her beauty in his statue of Fame.

The construction of the state monument came to a halt due to a disagreement between the sculptor and the commission. The Iowa commission and the War Department worried about future deterioration of the statues and staining of the stones from the bronze and thus required all bronze work on the monuments be made of U.S. standard bronze. Triebel cast all his bronzes in a foundry in Pistojo, Italy, and shipped them to the United States. When tested, the Italian bronzes did not have the same element mix as U.S. standard bronze. As a result, the committee rejected all the bronzes, except for the statue of Fame. Fame had the required mix of zinc and copper. The chairman of the committee, E.B. Soper, informed Triebel that he needed to recast all the rejected bronzes. Shocked, the sculptor educated the committee on the quality of Italian bronze. Soper, trying to work with the artist, replied that he would be willing to have an expert assess the bronzes, but the reason for the U.S. standard bronze was to prevent corrosion or rust on the granite. Aggravated that the artist was not willing to recast the bronzes, Soper also reminded Triebel that the requirement of U.S. standard bronze was in the contract and that he had agreed to it. Alarmed, Triebel informed the chairman that as an artist he had the liberty to better his design, as well as strengthen the construction. In his opinion, the Italian bronze was stronger due to the lower copper content.

The situation became frustrating for Triebel. He had already cast the bronzes and had them shipped from Italy to Pittsburg Landing for the monument. Because the monument was still not complete, the artist bore the expenses from his own pocket. Triebel, trying to support a family and concerned over expenses, requested to meet with the committee. Soper believed that a meeting would solve nothing and refused to grant his request. Desperate for payment, Triebel sent a cryptic telegram to Soper. The telegram simply read, "Reflect. Drastic measures taken. I offer these bronzes or none." Soper read the telegram to mean that Triebel would resort to drastic measures if the committee did not accept his bronzes. He sent a curt response to the sculptor informing him that the committee had asked him to live up to the contract and that he could not help that the artist's bills were due. Soper reminded Triebel that so far he had not delivered the monument by the date in the contract and that the committee would have every right to take drastic measures against him for breach of contract. He further warned the sculptor to "reflect carefully before you proceed to kick up a muss. The State can stand it, in the position which it holds, very much better than you can." Perhaps frightened, Triebel wrote back that there was a misunderstanding of the telegram. He never intended to take drastic measures and only wanted the committee to reflect on the drastic measures it had taken against him. The sculptor attempted to reason and smooth over the situation by chiding Soper, "Now don't you believe you have kept that American eagle captive long enough? I know he wants to get on top of that column and dominate the battlefield." He assured the chair that the committee would want to carry him "in triumph when you compare my work to those of any of the battlefield monuments."

To prove the quality of the Italian bronze, they further tested it. The bronzes remained in storage awaiting approval at Pittsburg Landing. Triebel and a commission member visited the park and sawed out two pieces of the bronze. They sent it to a Harvard professor, who tested the bronze pieces for corrosion, rust, staining and discoloration. The results concluded that the Italian bronze used by Triebel was as good as U.S. standard bronze. The committee accepted the statues.

The state of Iowa had erected monuments to its soldiers at Vicksburg, Chattanooga, Shiloh and Andersonville Prison. Governor Albert B. Cummins decided to take a grand tour through the South and dedicate all the monuments at once. The governor and his wife accompanied the battlefield commissioners, veterans and the Fifty-fifth Iowa regimental band on a two-week tour of the battlefields aboard a special train. After dedicating the monuments at Chattanooga, the group boarded a steamer in Paducah, Kentucky, and headed to Shiloh. Arriving on a Thursday, the group traveled in wagons and buggies around the battlefield dedicating the regimental monuments. At each one, the band played, invocation was said and a member of the regiment addressed the crowd. The next day, the crowd gathered around the impressive and inspiring Iowa Monument for its

Fifteenth Iowa Infantry veterans at the monument honoring their regiment at the Shiloh battlefield. *From left to right*: Captain I.B. Thatcher and wife, Major W.P.L. Muir and Major H.C. McArthur and wife. Circa 1906. *Photographer J.C. Donnell, Pittsburg Landing. Photo 5000.417, Special Collections, State Historical Society of Iowa, Des Moines.*

Members of the Iowa Monument Commission at the monument honoring the state's soldiers at the Shiloh battlefield, November 23, 1906. *Photographer J.C. Donnell, Pittsburg Landing. Photo 10042, Special Collections, State Historical Society of Iowa, Des Moines.*

In 1909, a cyclone ripped through the park, destroying park buildings, damaging trees and stones in the National Cemetery and damaging monuments. *Photo courtesy of the Shiloh National Military Park.*

Cyclone damage to the Iowa Monument in 1909. *Photo courtesy of the Shiloh National Military Park.*

dedication. After the ceremony, the group boarded the steamer to travel to Vicksburg and Andersonville.

In 1909, Mother Nature attempted to destroy the beautiful Iowa Monument. On October 14, a cyclone struck the park after ripping through the community of Mount Vinson west of the park. It traveled through the park in a flash, leaving a path of destruction. The large trees in the cemetery littered the ground in piles of twisted wood and debris. The majestic Iowa Monument, once towering above the park, lay in pieces on the ground. The storm violently ripped off one of Fame's arms and toppled the eagle. The park staff immediately began cleaning up the debris and assessing the damage to the monument. Calling on the federal government and the State of Iowa, they repaired the column and bronzes. A year later, Iowa's eagle flew high above the battlefield, and Fame continued to write on the pages of history.

Wisconsin

It embodies the beautiful and patriotic sentiment that all who die upon the battlefield for their country are sure of reward in heaven.
—*F.H. Magdeburg, speaking about the Wisconsin monument*

The sun shone brightly that April 7, 1906, as elderly men dressed in suits, their wives and others marched along the road to a large monument in the woods on the Shiloh battlefield. They had come to dedicate the Wisconsin Monument. After the speeches, poems and songs, the group took photos around the monument, walking around it and gazing up into the faces of the statue. When the group returned to its steamboat to return home, all parties agreed that it was a memorable day that honored the brave soldiers, and the monument would tell the story of the Union army at Shiloh to all future generations.

No doubt that as they crossed the peaceful fields and woods, the veterans' minds wandered back to their youths, when they had struggled to survive the fierce fighting on the very field they were now marching across. The Sixteenth Wisconsin, assigned to the Sixth Division under General Benjamin Prentiss, held off the first volleys from Confederate troops near Fraley Field at dawn. As the unit began moving back to Seay Field, a Rebel bullet hit Captain Edward Saxe of the Sixteenth Wisconsin, killing him. Saxe became the first Union officer killed in the fight. During the intense fighting on the first day, the regiments also lost six color-bearers.

Like the Sixteenth Wisconsin, the other two units were green recruits. Both the Fourteenth and the Eighteenth had mustered in 1862 and only recently arrived at Pittsburg Landing. The Fourteenth arrived with Buell's Army of the Ohio during the evening of April 6. The Eighteenth had arrived at Savannah, Tennessee, to report to General Grant. The general assigned the unit to Prentiss's division, and the troops traveled on to their campsite. Despite their lack of training, the Wisconsin soldiers served with Prentiss in the hornet's nest, holding their position for a large portion of the first day. During the two days of fighting, the people of Wisconsin lost 627 soldiers.

The Wisconsin Monument, by Robert Porter Bringhurst. *Photo by Jimmy and Jane Christopher.*

Above: Dedication of the Wisconsin Monument, April 1906. *Photo WHI-74226, Wisconsin Historical Society.*

Left: Captain Edward Saxe, the first officer killed during the Battle of Shiloh, April 6, 1862. *Photo from* Wisconsin at Shiloh: Report of the Commission *by F.H. Magdeburg.*

Thirty-nine years later, several of those surviving veterans worked to recognize these soldiers' actions with a monument at Shiloh. In 1901, D.B.G. James, the department commander of the Grand Army of the Republic and a veteran of the Sixteenth Wisconsin, and surgeon E.J. Buck of the Eighteenth Wisconsin prepared a bill asking for $20,000 to erect a monument in honor of the Wisconsin troops. The bill quickly passed, and the state legislature appropriated $10,000 "to commemorate the deeds and valor of its regiments which had taken part in the fight." Governor Robert Lafollette appointed Captain F.H. Magdeburg of the Sixteenth Wisconsin as chairman of the Wisconsin Shiloh Commission. Four other veterans of the battle readily accepted appointments to the commission as well.

The commissioners visited the park in 1913 to select the appropriate site and then sent out circulars calling for design submissions. To make the project more appealing, the committee offered the winning designer $250. A friend of Captain Magdeburg, another Wisconsin veteran, unofficially submitted a design. W.R. Hodges, a monuments dealer in St. Louis, worked with Magdeburg to create a monument that fit the idea that Magdeburg hoped to convey. Drawing from a monument he had seen in Germany, the captain wanted the world to know that all who died on a battlefield for their country would receive their just reward in heaven. Working with his friend Hodges, the two came up with a design and entered it in the competition. The committee unanimously agreed that this design would best represent and honor the Wisconsin soldiers.

Hodges, a monument maker, was not a sculptor and therefore could not sculpt the image requested by Magdeburg. Instead, he hired prominent St. Louis sculptor Robert Porter Bringhurst. The artist, like many sculptors, began his career working in the monument business. Wanting more challenge and to pursue finer sculpting and art, Bringhurst quit his work as a monument carver to study at the School of Fine Arts at Washington University. After a few years of study in St. Louis, Bringhurst moved to Paris to study at the famous École des Beaux-Arts. Inspired, challenged and improved as an artist, the sculptor moved back to St. Louis, where he took a job as a professor at his alma mater. Bringhurst enjoyed his teaching position and was busy with this work and entering various competitions when he received

Columbia and the soldier, by Robert Porter Bringhurst. *Photo by Jimmy and Linda Christopher.*

the commission for the Wisconsin Monument.

Hodges and Magdeburg envisioned a sculpture that represented a wounded color sergeant and the figure of Columbia grasping the flag from his dying hands. Both men and the committee agreed that the soldier should represent Captain Edward Saxe, the first officer killed in the battle. Magdeburg gave Bringhurst very specific instructions about how he wanted the figures to look. He suggested that the soldier should not be dead but mortally stricken. By grasping at his death wound near his heart, the soldier would express his agony. Magdeburg believed that the figure taking the flag represented Victory, thus showing the soldier that his effort and sacrifice for his country would be not in vain. Magdeburg argued that this would be clear to the soldier "by Victory holding aloft the flag carried, where in his last dying moments he can gaze upon it and glory in the comforting thought of Victory won." The sentimental captain suggested that the figure of Victory, as he preferred to call her, should be imposing and chaste, her face expressing tenderness and solitude.

The committee turned its attention to the rest of the monument's design. The artist's concept called for a six-foot-high and nine-foot, four-inch pedestal base for the sculpture. Charles A. Fink of Milwaukee, the architect designing the pedestal, added four low bas-reliefs to the design. The first panel represented the Fourteenth

Wisconsin capturing an artillery battery. The second relief depicted the opening of the fight by the Sixteenth Wisconsin, as well as the figure of Captain Saxe as he was falling and dropping his sword. The third bronze illustrated the fighting of the Eighteenth Wisconsin in the hornet's nest. The last panel included an inscription and the Wisconsin coat of arms.

The forty-fourth anniversary of the battle seemed the logical choice for the dedication. A large group of veterans, their families and Wisconsin dignitaries traveled by railroad and then

The face of Columbia, or Victory, by Robert Porter Bringhurst. *Photo by Jimmy and Linda Christopher.*

aboard the steamer *Saltillo* to Pittsburg Landing. Upon arrival, park personnel took the group on a tour of the battlefield. The family of Captain Edward Saxe was among the visitors, and the group paid homage to the captain by visiting the spot where he met his fate on April 6, 1862. The following day, the Wisconsin visitors ate breakfast aboard the steamer and then went ashore to march to the monument for the ceremonies. A Confederate reunion at Shiloh Church led many of the former Rebels to attend the dedication ceremonies. The former enemies greeted one another and reminisced. A Southerner greeted Judge Jacob Fawcett, saying, "I see you were with Prentiss's division." Fawcett replied that he was, indeed. The old Rebel stated that he was also there but on the other side. This prompted Fawcett

Left: Wisconsin veterans marching to their monument from Pittsburg Landing, circa 1906. *Photo from* Wisconsin at Shiloh: Report of the Commission *by F.H. Magdeburg.*

Below: The Wisconsin color-bearer's face, by Robert Porter Bringhurst. *Photo by Jimmy and Linda Christopher.*

to respond in jest that "maybe you are the son of a gun who shot me." The old Confederate laughed heartily and told the judge that he "shouldn't wonder, for I was trying hard enough to shoot some of you fellows at that time."

Ohio

Future generations coming here to look upon them learn brave history and will be persuaded by them to cultivate a love of country.
—*David F. Pugh, chairman of the dedication ceremonies for Ohio*

People scurried around the boat unloading cargo down the gangplank. The park employees watched anxiously as a crane lifted the first of the thirty-four granite Ohio monuments onto the train. Once it was secured with ropes, the engine was started, and the train began pulling the monument up from the landing to the top of the bluff. At the top, workers began unhooking the engine to start the process again. Once the stones reached the top, men worked quickly to hook up a team of horses to the wagon. The driver and seven other men followed along down the graded dirt road toward a spot in the hornet's nest. The first state regimental monument was ready to be set into place.

The monuments would pay tribute to the valor, sacrifice and actions of the Ohio soldiers at Shiloh on April 6 and 7, 1862. Ohio soldiers made up 22 percent of the Union army at Pittsburg Landing. They fought in the hornet's nest with Sherman and McClernand and arrived at the battlefield with Buell during the evening of April 6. The men of Ohio fought hard to force the Confederates off the battlefield the second day, thus securing the landing and saving the army. Ohio reported 1,955 casualties, making up 15 percent of the army's casualties. The state of Ohio had great reason to remember and honor its sons.

In 1898, Ohio governor Asa S. Bushnell appointed a group of Civil War veterans to form the Shiloh Battlefield Commission. After organizing, the group visited the battlefield in November 1898. After several days of going over the park locating Ohio battle lines with Cadle and Reed, the group returned home. Inclement weather had kept the men from completing their task, so they returned in April 1899. Wishing to make a wise choice and to gather ideas, the committee also visited the Gettysburg and Chickamauga battlefields. The commissioners returned and resolved to not use any bronze on their monuments. Cut lettering and carving would inscribe the deeds of their valiant men.

An Ohio regimental monument in the shape of a Minié ball. *Photo by Jane Beal.*

After locating battle lines, the question of how best to honor the Ohio veterans remained. The commission decided to erect a monument to each Ohio unit. In July 1900, notices went out in all newspapers in the principal cities in Ohio and New York City for design proposals. The response was overwhelming. Over 400 designs arrived by the deadline, representing some of the largest and most prestigious granite companies in the United States. The committee selected 134 designs and placed them on exhibit in the senate chamber of the statehouse in Columbus, Ohio, for one month. This allowed the public to view the proposals. By November 1900, the committee happily announced that it had not selected one design but rather a company. It had decided to hire Hughes Granite and Marble Company of Ohio. Each monument would be different and distinct. Through

the Grand Army of the Republic posts, a Union veteran organization, it announced to the survivors of the Battle of Shiloh that each regiment would have a monument erected on the battlefield. The commission would consult the veterans about what design and inscription they preferred.

For the Hughes Granite and Marble Company, this was a major project and award. Carmi Sandusky had founded the company in 1880, and four years later he added his brother-in-law, William E. Hughes,

Ohio Fourteenth Artillery Monument shortly after dedication. *Photo courtesy of the Shiloh National Military Park.*

Eighty-first
Ohio Infantry
Monument. *Photo
by Jane Beal.*

as a partner. Unfortunately, Carmi Sandusky died in 1893, leaving
Hughes to manage the business. The late nineteenth century proved
a booming time for the company. By 1890, Hughes employed fifty-
five master stonecutters, sculptors and engineers. As they toured the
Chickamauga battlefield, the Ohio commissioners probably did not
realize they were viewing work by the Hughes Granite Company.
Shiloh was only one of several battlefield contracts. There is some
reason to believe that a sculptor by the name of Loester created the
designs for the Ohio monuments. It is possible that he was a sculptor
in the employ of the Hughes Company.

After a lengthy controversy between the Eighty-first Ohio veterans
and the Shiloh Battlefield Commission over the position and actions
of the Eighty-first Ohio, the state was ready to dedicate its thirty-
four monuments. Ohio would be the first state to hold ceremonies

in honor of its sons on the battlefield. The commission set the date for June 6, 1902. On June 3, the commission, veterans and other delegates from Ohio boarded a railroad car headed to Paducah, Kentucky. There, they boarded the steamer *City of Memphis*, traveling the remaining 229 miles along the Tennessee River to Pittsburg Landing. An estimated two thousand people gathered in the bright sun and heat to witness the first dedication of a monument in the new park. Confederate colonel Josiah Patterson, a member of the Shiloh Commission, summed up the ceremony and feelings of all in his speech by saying, "By a common grief the North and South was welded into a more homogeneous nation."

Pennsylvania

A perpetual memorial to the fidelity of the soldiers.
—Pennsylvania Commission

The men slipped on their long black overcoats and put on their bowler hats. A few grabbed canes to help steady themselves. They were no longer young men. As they finished their conversation, they all agreed they must visit the Shiloh battlefield to determine the best place to erect a monument to the only regiment from Pennsylvania to serve in the bloody battle. On a chilly day in late November 1901, five members of the Pennsylvania Shiloh Commission toured the battlefield with park superintendent Cornelius Cadle, Shiloh commissioner Colonel Josiah Patterson and the park engineer. Accompanying the group on the tour was the famous general Lew Wallace. They reminisced about the war and occasionally had disagreements over events. At the end of the day, the group posed for a photo. The commission had developed ideas for the location of a memorial to the Seventy-seventh Pennsylvania.

The soldiers of the Seventy-seventh Pennsylvania were a long way from home in April 1862. The regiment had mustered into the army in October 1861. After mustering, the army attached them to General Don Carlos Buell's Army of the Ohio. On the morning of April 6, 1862,

Pennsylvania Monument, by Julius C. Loester. *Photo by Jimmy and Linda Christopher.*

The Pennsylvania Shiloh Commission visiting the battlefield. General Lew Wallace visited the battlefield at the same time, and the group posed with the famous general and author. General Wallace stands with a cane. The gentleman to his right is John Obreiter, after whom the statue on the Pennsylvania Monument is modeled. *Photo courtesy of the Shiloh National Military Park.*

the men found themselves thirty miles from where they were to join another large Union encampment. Sometime in the early morning, the command received orders to march double-quick to Savannah. Upon reaching the town, the men received orders to move quickly to Pittsburg Landing, where Grant's army was under attack. The Pennsylvanians embarked on a steamboat early the next morning and went upriver to the landing. They arrived terrified but ready to assist in forcing back the Confederates. The Pennsylvanians advanced and fought until they ran out of ammunition. During the long fight, the regiment charged a Confederate battery and captured two of the guns. They had earned their battle stripes during their first major engagement.

One member of the commission stated that they wished to erect a "perpetual memorial to the fidelity of the soldiers." The commission selected a site along Review Field for its monument. The task remained to find a design that told the story of the heroic Pennsylvanians at Shiloh. In 1901, they sent out circulars inviting monument builders from around the country to submit designs for consideration. After careful thought and screening, the commissioners chose a simple design by W. Liance Cottrell with the Harrison Granite Company of New York. Cottrell was a master carver who worked with the company for twenty years. He would carve and design the Vermont granite base.

The design called for a bronze soldier on top and bronze bas-reliefs along the side of the pedestal. The commission hired sculptor

Sketch of a proposed bronze relief by Julius C. Loester. *Courtesy of the Shiloh National Military Park.*

Bronze relief of the Seventy-seventh Pennsylvania charging an artillery battery. *Photo by Jane Beal.*

Julius C. Loester. The bronze soldier would be in uniform and have the equipment worn by soldiers at the battle. For his model, Loester used a photograph of commission chairman John Obreiter during the war. The chairman had been a color-bearer for the Seventy-

Bronze relief of the surrender on the Seventy-seventh Pennsylvania Monument. *Photo by Jane Beal.*

Artist sketch of the proposed bronze relief of the surrender by Julius C. Loester. *Courtesy of the Shiloh National Military Park.*

seventh during the battle. The bas-reliefs depicted principal events from the history of the regiment in the battle. One scene depicted the surrender of the colonel. The other relief depicted the regiment's heroic charge on an artillery battery.

With the completion of the monument, the State of Pennsylvania set a date for the dedication: November 12, 1903. Because the Pennsylvania Monument at Missionary Ridge was ready for dedication, the governor decided to make a journey to both battlefields. The state provided free transportation on the railways to the veterans of the Seventy-seventh who wished to travel to the dedication ceremonies. Almost one hundred citizens, along with Pennsylvania governor Samuel Pennypacker, traveled to Missionary Ridge. After dedicating the monument, the group boarded the steamer *Clyde* and traveled to Shiloh.

Minnesota

He is looking out upon the ground made glorious by immortal valor.
—Description of the Minnesota statue

It was only one battery, and it seemed that history would forget it. However, the veterans themselves could never forget the fierce fighting and struggle of those two days in April. General Benjamin

Minnesota Monument, by John Karl Daniels. *Photo by Jimmy and Linda Christopher.*

Prentiss corrected the records of April 6 to note that the only Minnesota troops in the battle fought valiantly in the hornet's nest. Munch's First Battery of Minnesota Light Artillery held off five Confederate assaults that day. The men from Minnesota would never forget the sights, smells and fear they experienced at Shiloh. Five officers and 121 men served in the battle, and three lost their lives.

Minnesota had only the one battery of artillery at the Battle of Shiloh. Though representation from the state seemed small compared to the numbers serving in other battles, the state legislature approved the formation of a monument commission in May 1907. It also appropriated $5,000 for a monument to the artillery battery. The commission sent out circulars to prominent artists and monument dealers in the United States inviting submissions. It took little

Model of the artillerist for the Minnesota Monument, by John Karl Daniels. *Minnesota Historical Society.*

discussion to select the design submitted by the P.N. Peterson Granite Company of St. Paul, Minnesota. The company's design was simple but powerful. It agreed to employ artist John Karl Daniels to sculpt the bronze statue of the artilleryman.

Daniels, an immigrant, was not old enough to have served in the war. Born in 1874, he immigrated to the United States with his family in 1884. While attending high school in St. Paul, Minnesota, he received formal training as a sculptor. He later moved to Norway to study under Knut Okerberg. He subsequently moved to Paris to study sculpture and, upon completion of his studies abroad, moved back to Minnesota. After his return, he accepted numerous commissions for the state capitol.

The Shiloh sculpture would be one of his more prominent works. The Peterson Granite Company designed the base to represent a sarcophagus made of Minnesota granite. The statue represented the average soldier, about twenty-two years of age. The committee believed that the soldier's face exhibited courage and mercy. He looked out on the ground "made glorious by immortal valor."

MICHIGAN

Let them become shrines for future generations of Americans—not that war may be glorified, but that courage may be commemorated.
—*From a speech at the Indiana dedication*

By 1907, most Northern states that had numerous troops in the battle had erected monuments. Many had acted within a few years after the formation of the park. Michigan still had not erected a monument to its valiant soldiers. It was not due to lack of interest by the veterans themselves. By 1907, many worried that they would never see a monument recording their actions for posterity. In 1894, the chair of the Michigan Shiloh Commission tried to introduce a bill for appropriations. Unfortunately, it never made it to the floor for presentation or a vote. Thirteen years later, Hiram Brown of the Michigan Twelfth Volunteer Infantry wrote to park historian David Reed. He updated the historian on his effort to get legislation

Michigan Monument. *Photo by Jimmy and Linda Christopher.*

passed and to rally support through newspapers. The tired old veteran suggested that the historian write to the governor of Michigan calling attention to the fact that the state had not honored its soldiers on the battlefield. Reed, understanding the concern and plight of the veteran, began a letter-writing campaign on behalf of the Michigan veterans. He pointed out that only Michigan and Nebraska had failed to honor their veterans.

Reed's efforts failed to garner support for a monument in 1907. The veterans, sensing they would never see a monument, continued to push for funding. In 1912, the Michigan Senate passed the bill, but the House adjourned and the bill failed. Finally, in 1916, after many Michigan veterans had answered the final roll call, a bill passed unanimously. The state chose a simple monument with a stock soldier on the top. On Memorial Day 1919, fifty-seven years after the battle, the remaining veterans gathered on the battlefield to dedicate their monument. This would be the last group of Union veterans to attend a dedication honoring them.

4

CONFEDERATE MONUMENTS

The men who struggled on this field are your heros—come here and build monuments to their glory, whether they wore the blue or the grey.
—Park superintendent Delong Rice, 1913

The former Confederate States of America dissolved at the end of the Civil War. Without a national government to expend funds to memorialize the deeds of its soldiers, the task fell to the individual Southern state governments and private organizations. Reconstruction left state economies struggling to regain strength. With very little extra funds available, only a few states erected monuments on key battlefields. Oddly enough, despite the size and significance of the Shiloh battle, Southern state governments did not erect monuments in the park. Memorializing the Confederate soldiers and perpetuating their memory became the priority of Southern women and a few individuals.

Bates's Second Tennessee

*It matters not whether his buried chivalry rests under the dry, smooth
surface of mother earth; under the little swelling mound of green, or
under the marble shaft—it is equally a patriot's rest and a hero's grave.
—"Old Comrades' Goodbye," by Captain Hampton Cheny, Second
Tennessee Regiment*

Great pride filled the audience members dressed in their finest hats,
suits and dresses. Birds chirped, and a slight breeze blew among
the trees. Captain Robert D. Smith, with great pride, introduced
the speaker for the dedication: Judge S.F. Wilson. Wilson, a former
Confederate soldier, stood up, his empty sleeve pinned to his coat.
He cleared his throat and began to give an address in honor of the
members of the Second Tennessee Regiment. After the comments,
Captain Hampton Cheny's beautiful young daughter unveiled the
monument. A photographer gathered the crowd around it and took
a picture to document the ceremonies for the first Confederate
monument dedicated in the park.

The Second Tennessee Infantry answered the call to arms of the
Confederacy very early in the war. A group of young men from
Sumner County, Tennessee, primarily under the age of twenty,
rushed to arms before their home state even joined the Confederacy.
Offering themselves to the Confederate government, they had the
distinction of being the first regiment accepted for a twelve-month
enlistment. After serving twelve months along the Potomac River,
the men received a sixty-day furlough. As they headed home, Fort
Donelson and Nashville fell to enemy hands. Instead of returning to
their homes, the Second Tennessee offered their services to General
Johnston in Corinth. Johnston organized them under Colonel William
B. Bates of Cleburne's brigade. Approximately 385 men entered
the battle on April 6. During the fighting, Colonel Bates received
a wound, and the regiment reported 235 men killed, wounded or
missing after the battle. The 65 percent casuality rate and the severe
fighting were burned into the memories of the surviving Tennessee
soldiers. As a result, they were the first Confederate group to erect a
monument on the battlefield.

Bates's Second Tennessee Monument. *Photo by Jimmy and Linda Christopher.*

Members of Bates's Second Tennessee gathered in front of their monument.
Courtesy of the Tennessee State Library and Archives.

Colonel Bates, who led the Tennesseans into battle that April, later honored his soldiers. In 1902, he began organizing a committee to erect a monument to his brave men. Six former members of the regiment began working to collect subscriptions from veterans, families and other interested Tennesseans. Although simple in design, the monument paid tribute to the men of Tennessee. A soldier ready to enter battle with a musket in hand adorned the top of the pedestal, and a Confederate flag and the letters "C.S.A." denoted the side for which the men had served. The other side of the pedestal listed the names of those killed in the battle. The third side included the name of the regiment and a quote from General Cleburne: "Go stranger, and tell Tennesseans that here we died for her. Tennesseans can never mourn for a more nobler band than fell this day in her 2nd Regiment."

With somber respect, the committee selected a date in October 1903 to dedicate the monument. Veterans and their families boarded the steamer *Kentucky* and traveled to the battlefield. After a long journey, the group disembarked and rode carriages across the park to the awaiting monument. The ceremonies paid tribute to General Johnston and the honor and noble cause for which the soldiers fought. They praised the government in its work to recognize both sides on the battlefield. After the speeches, the crowd left and returned home. Finally, someone had dedicated a monument to Southerners.

ALABAMA AND ARKANSAS

Could the dead speak, they would join their surviving comrades in proffers of gratitude. The sons of Alabama who fell upon this field, whose heroic spirits passed amid the smoke and thunder of battle, would have asked no greater reward for the service they so bravely rendered, no better recompense for the toil they endured, the danger they dared, and the gate they accepted in behalf of their native land, than the tribute they now receive from its daughters.
—Basil Duke's address at the Alabama Monument dedication

The Southern states' governments hesitated to erect monuments at the Shiloh National Military Park. Veterans and other concerned groups took the task to heart. During the early 1890s, women in the South began forming Confederate aid societies. In 1894, they consolidated, and in honor of Confederate president Jefferson Davis's daughter, Winnie Davis, they adopted the name United Daughters of the Confederacy (UDC). Preserving the memory of the Confederacy and honoring the Confederate veterans became their primary goal. In 1899, at the Richmond convention, the United Confederate Veterans asked the UDC to finish a monument it had started. Almost a decade later, the women unveiled the Jefferson Davis Monument—their first. They were now ready to raise funds for other memorials.

If it were not for the interest and push of the women, the states of Alabama and Arkansas would not have monuments at Shiloh National Military Park. Shortly after the creation of the park,

Commissioner Cadle wrote to the governors of each state with troops engaged in the battle. He informed them of the park's creation and encouraged each to erect a monument honoring the troops. In January 1899, Cadle wrote to the governor of Alabama pointing out that the commission was working with Alabama veterans and the state commission in marking positions. He suggested that the state create a monument commission. Unfortunately, the governor informed Cadle that the state legislature had taken no action.

The idea of an Alabama monument seemed to have disappeared in the state legislature. The women of Alabama carried on the idea. In February 1899, Mrs. L.G. Dawson made an appeal to her fellow United Daughters of the Confederacy to raise funds to erect a monument on one of the four battlefield parks. The women sent out the call for funds to all the chapters in Alabama and to the state's camp of United Confederate Veterans and Sons of Confederate Veterans. The women were persistent. After eight years, they had raised enough funds for the monument. During the May 1906 meeting in Eufaula, Alabama, the convention chose Shiloh as the site for the monument. After selecting a design, the UDC hired Morris Brothers of Memphis, Tennessee, to create the monument. The design was simple but elegant. A simple shaft with a pyramid of cannonballs crowned the top. The Confederate flag, a musket and a saber graced the front. By September 1906, the organization had submitted its design specifications to the park commission for approval. Wasting no time, it put a rush on the monument, requesting that the Morris Brothers complete it by April 1, 1907.

In May 1907, with great anticipation, Alabama Confederate veterans, members of the UDC, families and other dignitaries boarded a train and then a steamer to travel to the park. When they arrived, buggies, carriages and wagons awaited to carry them to the veiled monument. Ladies from the UDC deposited a box of papers into the foundation as part of the ceremony, and Mrs. J. Thompson presented the monument to the United States government. The women of Alabama had dedicated the first Southern state monument on the battlefield.

Like the women of Alabama, the Arkansas United Daughters of the Confederacy believed that their soldiers should have some

Alabama Monument.
Photo by Jimmy and Linda Christopher.

Arkansas Monument.
Photo by Jimmy and Linda Christopher.

Statue on the Arkansas monument. *Photo by Jane Beal.*

type of monument on the Shiloh battlefield. The men of Arkansas, along with other Southern troops, had made many desperate attacks on the hornet's nest and eventually helped to capture the Union troops there. The various chapters of the Arkansas UDC collected funds to commission a simple monument at the park. A Confederate soldier peering into the haze of battle stood on the top. A pedestal detailed the courage and valor of the Arkansas men.

After raising the funds, the women commissioned the Morris Brothers of Memphis to create their monument. As the Morris Brothers worked, the Arkansas UDC began planning the dedication. The women worked with the park historian to select the most appropriate site: the center of the hornet's nest. They believed this spot best honored the gallantry of the Arkansas men during the battle. After much conferring with park officials about an opening in the base for relics and the display of a Confederate flag, the women selected September 6, 1911, for their ceremonies. When the day arrived, veterans, women and children gathered for the unveiling and speeches by Shiloh Confederate veteran Colonel Robert Shaver and others. Shiloh had another monument honoring the boys in gray.

United Daughters of the Confederacy Monument

As a greeting to its living remnant, and in honor of its dead—whether sleeping in distant places, or graveless here, in traceless dust—this moment of strength and beauty has been lifted up by the hands of a loving and grateful nation.
—Part of the proposed inscription for the UDC Monument

Many years would pass before the South would see another monument dedicated in its honor on the battlefield. After the park commission dissolved, the War Department hired a park superintendent to oversee park operations. DeLong Rice made it his mission to have a monument from every state that sent soldiers into battle. He lobbied all the Southern governors and legislatures to consider funding monuments. He hoped they would not forget the sacrifices and valor at Shiloh. Unfortunately, most states informed Rice that they believed their men needed to be recognized, but it was not in the state budgets.

Death Overcomes Victory, the Confederate monument by Frederick C. Hibbard, circa 1919. *Photo by Jimmy and Linda Christopher.*

Cornelia Irwin, founder of the Shiloh chapter of the UDC and promoter of the UDC Monument. *Photo courtesy of the Hardin County Historical Society.*

In March 1900, Cornelia Irwin, the wife of Captain James W. Irwin, organized the Shiloh chapter of the United Daughters of the Confederacy in the historic town of Savannah, Tennessee, with the sole purpose of erecting a monument "to the Confederate soldiers living and dead and especially for those who fell on the bloody field of Shiloh." Cornelia's husband worked for the park commission as the land agent. He had served with the Confederate army and acted as a guide for Beauregard during the Battle of Shiloh. Her heart broke at the thought that a monument did not honor the brave Rebels and serve as a permanent reminder of their deeds. Cornelia held the first meeting in her home, with twenty-six women becoming charter members.

Irwin and the other women began working toward funding a memorial. As they collected funds, they pitched their project to the Tennessee Division of the UDC. The state division agreed to assist in the project and to contribute twenty-five dollars each year until completion. In 1902, the state appointed a committee to oversee the project. In 1905, Mrs. Alexander White, the president of the Tennessee UDC, brought the project before the national convention in San Francisco. The national organization agreed to the project

Captain James Irwin, his wife Cornelia and their family. *Photo courtesy of the Hardin County Historical Society.*

Model of the Confederate monument by Frederick C. Hibbard. *Courtesy of the Shiloh National Military Park.*

and the following year established a committee to direct the work. The women decided that the memorial should cost $50,000. Women all across the state sold chickens and solicited funds in their communities and at veteran gatherings. They challenged children to save their pennies and donate them to the cause. Nine years later, the women proudly announced that they had collected the funds and were ready to dedicate a monument to their brave soldiers.

The women selected Frederick C. Hibbard as the artist for their monument. Although born after the war, Hibbard would capture the South's feelings toward the Battle of Shiloh and its loss. Born in 1881, in Canton, Missouri, the artist began his education as an engineer at the University of Missouri. He later moved to Chicago to study at the Armour Institute of Technology. However, his interests and passion were not in engineering, and he gave up his job and enrolled at the Art Institute of Chicago. This gave him the opportunity to study under the great sculptor Lorado Taft. After a year, Taft selected the talented sculptor to work as his assistant. By 1904, Hibbard had opened his own studio in Chicago. The United Daughters of the Confederacy may have selected Hibbard based on his work on the Illinois Monument at the Vicksburg National Military Park. The Confederate monument at Shiloh would become one of his largest and most impressive commissions.

The women wasted no time in preparing for the monument. In January 1915, Mrs. Alexander and the rest of the committee agreed to lay the cornerstone of the massive monument in a special ceremony on dedication day: May 30, 1916. Unforeseen problems with the production of the monument created a delay, and the women moved the cornerstone laying to November. With great celebration, they invited the Masonic lodge in Adamsville, Tennessee, to lay the cornerstone. The Masons began the ceremony by performing their ancient rites. The head of the committee gave a short address and laid a box with items significant to the project and the Confederacy inside the monument's base.

The box placed in the cornerstone contained a copy of the poem "Heroes of Gray"; a report and address of Mrs. Alexander B. White; memorial addresses from Confederate general George W. Gordon and Robert Love Taylor; flags from the UDCs in Tennessee and

Mississippi; a lock of General Albert Sidney Johnston's hair that had been taken from his head in Corinth after his death; lists of members of the Shiloh Committee, the design committee, the inspection committee, the Mississippi State Shiloh Committee, officers of the Corinth UDC and president generals of the UDC since the project began; a photograph of Dr. C. Kendrick and J.S. McFall in full Ku Klux Klan uniforms; a replica of the Confederate seal; coins from 1906 and 1916; a history of the organization of the Shiloh chapter of the UDC with a roster of its members; a photograph of the monument and its groups; a photograph of sculptor Frederick C. Hibbard; a history of the monument by Mrs. Alexander B. White; a sketch of the monument by the *St. Louis Post Dispatch*; a report from the Shiloh Committee treasurer in 1916; a photograph of Captain J.W. Irwin; and a copy of the inscriptions on the monument.

The cornerstone ceremony only heightened the excitement. The women had planned to hold the dedication ceremony in the fall of 1916, but unforeseen events had delayed it. Before the cornerstone ceremony, the large granite stones that created the base of the monument were shipped to the park for the cornerstone laying. At the Mount Airy, Tennessee quarry, workers loaded the stones onto a railway car to ship to Danville along the Tennessee River. Upon arrival at Pittsburg Landing, large derricks lifted the stones from the boat, and then workers rolled or pulled the stones on large timbers up the landing and across the park. White reported to her fellow Daughters that "a friend wrote me that the Shiloh monument was stretching all the way with stones on the side of the roadway from the landing to Prentiss circle." With each stone weighing twenty-three tons, the task was slow-going but worth it. Rice reported to the women that the monument, even without the bronzes, was "beautiful and imposing, and will fulfill your highest expectations." Everything seemed ready for dedication when Hibbard informed the committee that the bronze foundry in Chicago had gone on strike, and it would be several weeks before they would be ready. This caused a postponement of the dedication. At the annual meeting, White reassured the women that the wait would be well worth it. She had visited Hibbard's studio and had viewed the wax model of the central group: *Death Overcomes Victory*. Detailing the beauty of

Death Overcomes Victory, the central figures on the Confederate monument. The center figure represents Victory or the Confederacy. The other figures represent Night and Death. *Photo by Jimmy and Linda Christopher.*

the bronze, White explained that she wanted the women to see "the wonderful drapery and how arms show through it; see the poise and grace of the figure Victory or Confederacy as everyone calls it."

As the foundry began working on casting the bronzes, Hibbard began working with the park superintendent on how best to transport the large and heavy bronze sculptures. The monument would have a total of three. The central bronze figure alone weighed three tons. Hibbard asked if there would be any problems sending the bronzes by train to Corinth and then hauling them by wagon to the park. Rice informed the sculptor that the bridges between the park and Corinth would not withstand such a heavy load; it would be best to ship by train and then transfer and ship them by steamer. A derrick would have to lift the bronzes from the steamer, and then another large derrick would lift the sculptures into place on the monument base. The entire monument weighed 242,200 pounds.

The entire park and the women of the Shiloh chapter of the UDC buzzed with excitement as the day for the dedication neared. This would be one of the largest dedication ceremonies held in the park. Finally, on May 17, the crowds entered the park by steamer and buggies. They gathered at the park pavilion to listen to the invocation speeches by the governor and members of the UDC. Mrs. Edger Cherry of the Shiloh chapter read the contents placed in the cornerstone, and Saxby's Band from Memphis, Boy Scouts and Campfire Girls led the crowd on a mile-long parade to the veiled monument. The crowd held their breaths as Mrs. Alexander White unveiled the

Model of the Confederate Monument's central figures, by Frederick C. Hibbard. *Courtesy of the Shiloh National Military Park.*

monument. Applause erupted, and a twenty-one-gun salute sounded as the band played taps. The son of General Nathan Bedford Forrest declared that it was the most beautiful monument he had ever seen.

Artist Frederick Hibbard came before the crowd to explain the monument he called *Death Overcomes Victory*. In the center of the pedestal, Hibbard had carved the bust of Confederate general Albert Sydney Johnston in low relief. Along the right side, also in low relief, twelve heads of men marched across the stone. These represented the Confederates coming into battle. On the opposite side, the men returned from battle with heads bowed—this represented the Confederates retreating in defeat. Three bronzes graced the top of the monument. The four figures on the ends represented the

Above: Confederate Monument, carving by Frederick C. Hibbard. The Confederate soldiers' heads are bowed in defeat. On the opposite side, Hibbard carved the heads up as they headed into battle. *Photo by Jimmy and Linda Christopher.*

Left: The Confederate Monument, cavalryman and officer, by Frederick C. Hibbard. *Photo by Jimmy and Linda Christopher.*

The Confederate Monument, artillerist and infantryman. *Photo by Jimmy and Linda Christopher.*

four branches of army service: artillery, infantry, cavalry and the general officer. The cavalryman, with his hand spread, indicated his frustration. He wanted to help but could not penetrate the heavy undergrowth. An officer stood behind him with his head bowed in submission to the cease-fighting order. On the opposite side stood the infantryman holding the flag in defeat in one hand and his musket in the other. Behind him stood the artillerist, ready to fight and peering through the haze.

Hibbard went on to explain the central figures. Here, three shrouded women stood representing Defeated Victory. The front figure, modeled after a young Kentucky woman, was Victory or the Confederacy. In grief, she handed over the laurel wreath of victory

The Confederate Monument, Victory handing the laurel wreath to Night and Death. *Photo by Jimmy and Linda Christopher.*

Dedication of the UDC Confederate Monument, 1917. *Photo courtesy of John Ross.*

to Death on her left and Night on her right. Hibbard explained that Death had come to their commander and Night had brought reinforcements to the enemy; thus, the Confederacy lost the battle. After the sculptor explained the symbolism of his monument, women laid wreaths, a closing prayer ended the ceremony and the band played once again. The crowd, estimated to be between two and three thousand, milled around the monument, took photographs and admired the beautiful work honoring the Southern soldiers' courage at Shiloh.

Louisiana

It matters not to me that I be known as its donor (for after all, what matters it, when all are dead, forgotten and unknown) but I do care that the state, or rather its politicians, be not credited with the performance of a duty that should but has not been performed.
—Dr. Yves R. Lemonnier to David Reed, July 1913

While the women of the United Daughters of the Confederacy were busy raising funds for their monument, a former Louisiana private began investigating the erection of a monument. In November 1913, Secretary Reed received a letter from a Dr. Yves R. Lemonnier informing him that he would like to erect a monument to the Crescent Regiment. He hoped to place it in the wheat field where he had fought on the second day of battle. Reed, delighted at the interest, responded with information on monument regulations and a copy of his history of the battle.

Lemonnier had been a private during the Civil War in the Louisiana Crescent Regiment from New Orleans. During the Battle of Shiloh, the regiment joined other Confederates as they closed in around General Prentiss's troop in the hornet's nest. Approximately 42 percent of the Crescent Regiment died during the two days of fighting. After the war, Lemonnier returned to his hometown of New Orleans, where he studied and practiced medicine. In 1882, the governor of Louisiana appointed him coroner for the city of New Orleans, a position he served in until his retirement in 1900.

107

Louisiana Crescent Regimental Monument, by Albert Weiblen. *Photo by Jimmy and Linda Christopher.*

When not studying medicine, he studied the Battle of Shiloh. Lemonnier published a book defending Louisiana general P.G.T. Beauregard's reputation in the battle. During this time, he decided that his former regiment should be recognized and honored.

It is unclear if Lemonnier attempted to solicit funds from fellow veterans, the state or other citizens. No records appear of his asking for funding assistance. He gave the impression that he was unable to gain the sympathy and assistance of his local and state politicians, thus leaving him bitter toward them and their treatment of the Confederate veterans. The local veteran organizations focused their attention and money on the Confederate monument in Richmond and the Louisiana monument in Vicksburg. Lemonnier seemed to feel that his fellow veterans were forgetting the Battle of Shiloh and that future generations would forget these soldiers' sacrifice. By erecting the monument himself, he hoped to stimulate others to do likewise.

Being the sole supporter, the selection of the monument was Lemonnier's choice. By July 1912, he had selected Albert Weiblen of the Weiblen Monument and Granite Company to design a modest and simple memorial. The stone carver, a German emigrant, created many of the elegant tombs and memorials in New Orleans's cemeteries. He had won the commission for the reunion memorial arch, the North Carolina state monument and the Louisiana state monument at Vicksburg National Military Park.

Despite this not being his largest monument, Weiblen gave it his utmost care and consideration. A crescent moon shaped one side of the monument. Crossed muskets covered by a laurel graced the front. Because the exact number of men who went into battle could not be determined, the inscription on the front gave very basic information about the regiment. The design pleased Lemonnier, and he eagerly looked forward to its erection in the park. In June 1913, he wrote to Reed saying that his fellow comrades suggested that he receive recognition on the monument. The doctor, not wishing to take glory from the heroism of his regiment, suggested that the inscription on the back simply note that a private from Company B had erected the memorial. Lemonnier told Reed that "it matters not to me that I be known as its donor (for after all, what matters it, when all are dead, forgotten and unknown) but I do care that the state, or rather its politicians, be not credited with the performance of a duty that should but has not been performed."

As Weiblen worked on the monument, Lemonnier began trying to gather people to travel to Tennessee for the dedication. By 1915, his health had begun to decline, and his eyes had started to give him trouble. He informed the park that he would not be traveling with the monument company to see the installation. Sadly, he believed he would not find interested parties to attend a dedication. Lemonnier stated that "interested parties are too apathetic on the subject." The doctor set May 31, 1915, for the dedication of his monument. Unfortunately, his health precluded him from traveling to the park for the ceremony. Two years later, he wrote to the park to confirm that there were still only three Southern monuments at the park, as reported in the *Confederate Veteran*. Disheartened by the news, Lemonnier lamented the fact, saying, "It is a shame that the South is not more deservingly represented in our National Military Parks."

THE WHEELER MONUMENT

After the erection of the Confederate Monument by the UDC, monument building seemed to be at an end. Despite Superintendent Rice's efforts to encourage Southern state legislatures to erect memorials, nothing happened. In 1930, the park superintendent, Robert A. Livingston, received a letter from the General Joseph Wheeler Memorial Association in Alabama. It requested permission to erect a monument in honor of the general.

The park commission did not approve of monuments in honor of individuals. However, the commission and the early park founders were long gone. A new era had entered the park. Many of the stringent rules and beliefs changed with the younger generation. Livingston approved of the monument to Wheeler. General Joseph

The General Joseph Wheeler Monument, circa 1930. *Photo by Jane Beal.*

Wheeler had served with the Nineteenth Alabama under General Braxton Bragg during the battle and as the senior cavalry officer for the Army of Tennessee in the western theater. After the war, he served with the United States Army in the Spanish-American War and the Philippine War. He also represented the state of Alabama in the House of Representatives. Wheeler died in 1906.

The association erected a simple granite stone with rock face panels. Originally, the group had submitted an inscription that praised General Wheeler. The inscription read, "The superb gallantry, intrepid courage and unusual military ability of the boy soldier commanding this regiment contributed largely to the victory forces on the first day of battle, Sunday, April 6, 1862." This did not meet guidelines for inscriptions on monuments. The superintendent requested that the association change it. In response, the association submitted a simpler inscription that left out the praise and gave basic information about Wheeler and his command. In October 1930, the group traveled from Huntsville, Alabama, to the park and dedicated the monument. General Wheeler's daughter, Annie Wheeler, unveiled the stone before the crowd.

Texas and Kentucky

Though defeated, the Southern courage left immortal footprints on this field, and worn fadeless laurels form this torn and cannon splintered forest.
—DeLong Rice to the governor of Florida, 1913

The old soldiers would be long gone and their children would be elderly before another monument dedication occurred on the battlefield. The centennial of the war during the early 1960s sparked a renewed interest in the old battlefields. Historians released new books, and Americans began revisiting the parks. Once again, the states became interested in recognizing their contributions to the war. Many established historical commissions for the sole purpose of marking and honoring the deeds of their ancestors.

Texas State Monument. *Photo by Jane Beal.*

The centennial sparked a renewed interest in the Civil War in the states of Texas and Kentucky. Park superintendent DeLong Rice had requested that Texas erect a monument in 1913. The governor at the time responded that the state constitution did not allow for the funding of memorials outside the state. In 1963, John Ben Sheppard, the president of the Texas State Historical Survey Commission, suggested erecting a monument honoring Texans in the Battle of Shiloh. He informed the park superintendent that the citizens of his state wished to erect a marker some place where Texans had acquitted themselves favorably. In 1964, the state dedicated a simple red granite stone with a laurel wreath framing a lone star.

Kentucky, also motivated by the centennial, erected a monument in 1971. Wanting to use material that would withstand the test of time and modern technology, the state decided on an aluminum monument. Two pillars made of Kentucky marble embedded in

Kentucky State Monument. *Photo by Jane Beal.*

concrete held up an aluminum plaque ten feet long and five feet high. The plaque simply displayed a map of the battlefield on one side and the story of the battle and Kentucky's role in it on the opposite side. In 1989, the pilasters suffered damage due to improper curing and freezing. The state replaced the Kentucky granite with Georgia granite.

MISSOURI

Yes, give me the land where the battle's red blast
Has flashed to the future fame of the past;
Yes give me the land that hath legends and lays
That tell of the memories of long vanished days.
—*"A Land without Ruins," by Abram Joseph Ryan*

In June 1975, fourteen Boy Scouts and three leaders left St. Louis, Missouri, to hike a series of Civil War battlefields in the South. As

IN MEMORY OF HER SONS
WHO FOUGHT AND DIED
TO PRESERVE THOSE FREEDOMS
IN WHICH THEY BELIEVED
BATTLE OF SHILOH
APRIL 6TH AND 7TH 1862

Back of the Missouri State Monument. *Photo by Jane Beal.*

the boys hiked the Shiloh battlefield, they admired and studied the various monuments that dotted the fields. It soon became apparent as they crisscrossed the park going through the woods and fields that their home state of Missouri did not have a monument. Upon inquiring at the visitors' center, they were disappointed to learn that their observation was correct. Missouri had soldiers in both the Union and the Confederate armies during the battle, and yet neither side was given recognition.

After returning home to St. Louis, scout master John Leon began investigating how to get funding for a Missouri monument. He had no luck with the state legislature, so he began to appeal to the local veterans' organizations. After years of bake sales, car washes and presentations, Leon and the Boy Scouts raised $8,000 for a monument. With careful consideration, the group decided on a design that would honor Missouri soldiers who served on both sides. Selecting a design in the shape of the state, they chose different colors of granite for symbolism. The Mount Airy gray granite made up the state, but a pedestal of red Missouri granite and Norwegian

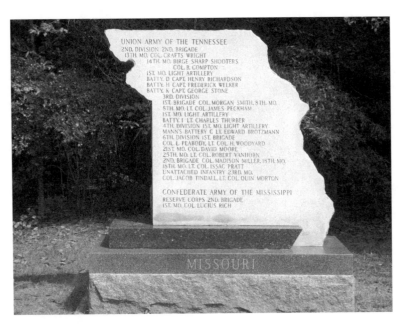

Missouri State Monument. This is the first monument to honor both Northern and Southern soldiers. *Photo by Jane Beal.*

blue granite held the state structure high. The gray stood for the Confederate soldiers and the blue for the Union. The red granite represented the total sacrifice of all the Missouri troops. On the back, they included a drawing of a hornet's nest. With pride of accomplishment, the Boy Scouts dedicated their monument to the soldiers of Missouri on May 17, 1981.

TENNESSEE STATE MONUMENT

As you have expressed, a memorial to Tennessee's Shiloh participants should be one of suitable symbolism, material and stature to demonstrate to all the state's pride in its heritage.
—Superintendent Woody Harrell to Bettye Stanley, September 1997

By the twenty-first century, it seemed as though the park was finished with dedicating monuments. The battle had occurred over one

Passing of Honor, Tennessee State Monument, by Gerald Sanders, 2005. *Photo by Jane Beal.*

hundred years earlier. Now the distant descendants of the veterans walked the battlefield; the Sons of the Confederate Veterans and the United Daughters of the Confederacy could aptly be renamed the Great-great-grandsons and Granddaughters of the Confederacy. The monuments erected to the Union troops were celebrating 100th anniversaries, and the Southerners finally had a few monuments on the battlefield. Oddly enough, though, Tennesseans still did not have a state monument.

Park visitors often remark how odd it was that the state in which the battle was fought did not erect a monument. The state of Tennessee sent the most troops into the battle. Locals joined both armies while they were encamped in the area and fought in the battle. Yet their deeds remained unnoticed and unremembered in stone or bronze. One area citizen and lifelong member of the UDC resolved to correct this oversight. Bettye Stanley, a member of the Shiloh chapter of the UDC, followed in the footsteps of Cornelia Irwin and began raising funds for a Tennessee state monument in 1992. Stanley and other members of the UDC traveled to Nashville to appeal to Governor Ned McWhorter for funding. This was unsuccessful. Determined, she began visiting UDC and Sons of Confederate Veterans chapter meetings and any other organization that might have an interest. With the support of the state division of the UDC and a committee created to head the project, the women visited with state representative Randy Rinks and state senator Steve McDaniel for assistance. McDaniel had been instrumental in getting a monument for the state of Tennessee erected on the Gettysburg battlefield. If the state could have a monument erected in Pennsylvania, surely it

Passing of Honor, by Gerald Sanders. The Tennessee soldier keeps a watchful eye over the battlefield. *Photo by Jane Beal.*

would help erect one at home. This time, their appeals were successful. Rinks and McDaniel managed to secure $125,000 for the project. The Sons of Confederate Veterans (SCV) now joined the efforts, donating money and working to find a design.

Tennessee needed a monument that stood out and represented the gallantry and sacrifice of its sons. The SCV and the UDC put out a call for artist submissions. Twelve different artists submitted designs. They ranged from contemporary in style to the simple. SCV president Jerry Lessenberry had recently seen a piece of art by a Texas artist, Gerald L. Sanders. Admiring his work, Lessenberry recommended that the group contact Sanders for a design.

117

Artist Gerald Sanders sculpting the uniform of a Confederate soldier in the wax mold for the Tennessee State Monument. *Photo courtesy of the Shiloh National Military Park.*

Sanders, a navy veteran of World War II and Korea, accepted the task. The Texas native had worked for Southwestern Bell for thirty-five years before retiring and becoming a full-time artist. At the time Lessenberry contacted him, Sanders had seen one of his sculptures honored. Inspired by his work with the telephone company, he created a sculpture honoring the lineman. Southwestern Bell loved the piece and featured it on its phonebook. Fourteen and a half million people had viewed Sanders's artwork. The Shiloh piece would be his largest sculpture.

Sanders decided to focus on the color-bearers. These men held the flag so that the soldiers fighting could follow it into battle and keep their battle line. The SCV had earlier tried to erect a monument to the Sixth Tennessee. The regiment had lost almost a dozen color-bearers during the assault on the hornet's nest. The monument never came to fruition. Inspired by this story, Sanders went to work sculpting the soldiers in wax.

Unlike the monuments created at the turn of the twentieth century, this monument would not have allegorical figures. The sculpture would be detailed and true to life. The monument, titled *Passing of Honor*, featured three soldiers. One soldier, the flag bearer,

Artist Gerald Sanders with the wax mold for the Tennessee State Monument.
Photo courtesy of the Shiloh National Military Park.

had fallen in battle. The second soldier picked up the flag to help carry on the fight. The third soldier kept watch. Park historian Stacy D. Allen and Fred Prouty, a military site advisor for the Tennessee Historical Commission, traveled to Sanders's studio to advise the artist on uniforms, equipment and accoutrements. After the clay models were completed, a foundry cast the nine-foot figures in bronze. Advances in metallurgy allowed Sanders to add color to the sculpture. He used stainless steel in the stars on the flag to add contrast to the bronze.

Park staff and local residents buzzed with excitement as the project neared completion. This would be the largest monument created since the Confederate Monument in 1917. Park officials worked with the UDC and the SCV in planning and preparing for the dedication. Park staff began preparing for the moving and erection of the monument. A steamboat had brought in the last monument of this size, and logs had rolled the granite blocks up the landing. Ninety years later, a truck and trailer would deliver the black Tennessee granite base and bronze figure. Instead of a derrick lifting the sculpture into place, a crane would lift it up and set it in place.

Left: Park superintendent Woody Harrell inspects the bronze sculpture of the Tennessee Monument on the trailer. *Photo courtesy of the Shiloh National Military Park.*

Below: Park staff watch as a crane lowers the bronze sculpture onto the pedestal for the Tennessee State Monument. *Photo courtesy of the Shiloh National Military Park.*

Park superintendent Woody Harrell followed in the footsteps of his predecessors in preparing for the dedication ceremonies. This would be the largest dedication ceremony since the UDC's. Locals buzzed with excitement. After putting the monument in place at Water Oaks Pond, the park covered it, and local reenactors provided a guard. Besides park staff and UDC and SCV members, no one would see the monument until its unveiling. On June 3, 2005, traditionally Confederate Memorial Day, hundreds of people gathered at the park. Senator McDaniel, the park superintendent and representatives of the UDC and SCV gathered to give speeches and honor Tennessee's Civil War heroes. Governor Phil Bresden presented the monument to the federal government, and a group of children pulled the cord and unveiled the long-awaited Tennessee State Monument.

EPILOGUE

O ver one hundred years ago, a group of veterans gathered to preserve the battlefield that had changed their lives and where they had lost their innocence. They gathered numerous times to dedicate monuments, hoping that future generations would not forget their story. Today, almost half a million people visit the battlefield yearly and gaze upon their monuments. As the years pass, younger generations often miss their significance. As a result, the park has battled vandalism for years. Thieves stole the star from the Texas Monument. Park staff worked with the State of Texas to replace it and even held a special ceremony honoring the return of the Lone Star. Vandals also took the bronze shield from the Johnston Mortuary Monument. Other monuments have suffered vandalism as well. Smaller parts of reliefs have broken or been vandalized. By the 1980s, the National Park Service had begun studying and developing the best methods for cleaning and preserving the monuments, thus creating a preservation plan. Today, time, patience and skill combat the ill effects of vandals, environment and age.

The monuments, often overlooked, are a testament to the dedication of the veterans. They are more than stone and bronze. The monuments are the veterans' attempt to tell their story for all of posterity. One only has to gaze into the face of Victory on the Confederate Monument to see the love and beauty of the old soldiers. As visitors read the inscriptions and admire the sculptures, they can hear the whispers of the veterans telling the story of the battle and pleading for remembrance and honor.

BIBLIOGRAPHY

Allen, Stacy D. "Shiloh! The Campaign and First Day's Battle." *Blue and Gray* (Winter 1997): 7–64.

Bolotin, Norman. *The Chicago's World Fair of 1893: The World's Columbian Exposition*. Washington, D.C.: National Trust for Historic Preservation, 1992.

Brooklyn Museum of Art. *The American Renaissance, 1876–1917*. New York: Pantheon Books, 1979.

City Art Museum. "City Art Museum of St. Louis: An Exhibition by Mr. Robert Porter Bringhurst and Mr. Frederick Oakes Sylvester." In *Exhibition Catalogue*. St. Louis: City Art Museum, 1911.

Cooley, Adelaide. *The Monument Maker: A Biography of Frederick Ernst Triebel*. Hicksville, NY: Exposition Press, 1978.

Coons, John W. *Indiana at Shiloh: Report of the Commission*. Indianapolis, IN: William B. Burford Press, 1904.

Cunningham, O. Edward. *Shiloh and the Western Campaign of 1862*. Edited by Gary D. Joiner and Timothy B. Smith. New York: Savis Beatie, 2007.

Daniel, Larry J. *Shiloh: The Battle that Changed the Civil War*. New York: Simon and Schuster, 1997.

Davis, Steve. *Johnny Reb in Perspective: The Confederate Soldier's Image in the Southern Arts*. Atlanta, GA: Emory University, 1979.

Eisenchimel, Otto. *The Story of Shiloh.* Chicago: Civil War Roundtable, 1946.

Fitts, Deborah. "Shiloh Prepares for June 3 Dedication of Tennessee Monument." *Civil War News,* May 2005.

Gillis, Joe. *The Confederate Monument Shiloh National Military Park.* N.p., 1994.

Hallmark, Richard Parker. *Chicago Sculptor Richard W. Bock: Social and Artistic Demands at the Turn of the Twentieth Century.* PhD diss., St. Louis University, 1980.

A History of Tennessee from the Earliest Times to the Present, together with an Historical and a Biographical Sketch of Shelby County. Nashville, TN: Goodspeed Publishing Co., 1887.

Johnson, Robert Underwood, ed. *Battles and Leaders of the Civil War: Being for the Most Part Contributions by Union and Confederate Officers.* Vol. 1. New York: Castle, 1956.

Lemonnier, Yves Reni. *General Beauregard at Shiloh.* New Orleans, LA: Graham Press, 1913.

Libretto, Ellen. Interview by Stacy Reaves, June 2011.

Lindsey, T.J. *Ohio at Shiloh.* Cincinnati, OH: C.J. Krehbiel and Co., 1903.

Lowe, William C. "A Grand and Patriotic Pilgrimage: The Iowa Civil War Monuments Dedication Tour of 1906." *Annals of Iowa* 69, no. 1 (Winter 2010): 1–50.

Magdeburg, F.H. *Wisconsin at Shiloh. Report of the Commission.* Milwaukee, WI: Riverside Printing Co., 1909.

Marten, Donald. *Masters of American Sculpture: The Figurative Tradition from the American Renaissance to the Millenium.* Abbeyville, OH: Abbeyville Press, 1930.

Marten, James. *Sing Not War: The Lives of Union and Confederate Veterans During the Gilded Age.* Chapel Hill: University of North Carolina, 2011.

Mason, George. *Illinois at Shiloh: Report of the Commission and Ceremonies at the Dedication of the Monuments Erected to the Positions of the Illinois Commands Engaged in the Battle.* Chicago: M.A. Donahue and Co., 1904.

Matas, Rudolph. *History of Medicine in Louisiana.* Baton Rouge: Louisiana State Press, 1958.

McCullough, David. *The Greater Journey: Americans in Paris.* New York: Simon and Schuster, 2011.

McDonough, James Lee. *Shiloh: In Hell Before Night.* Knoxville: University of Tennessee Press, 1977.

McPherson, James. *The Battle Cry of Freedom: The Civil War Era.* New York: Ballantine Books, 1988.

Pierre, Dorathi Bock, ed. *Memoirs of an American Artist: Sculptor Richard W. Bock.* Los Angeles: C.C. Publishing, 1989.

Poppenheim, Mary B. *The History of the United Daughers of the Confederacy.* Richmond, VA: Garrett and Massie, Inc., 1925.

Roland, Charles P. *Albert Sydney Johnston: Soldier of Three Republics.* Austin: University of Texas, 1964.

Sandusky County. *The Sandusky County Scrapbook.* http://www.sandusky-county-scrapbook.net/default.htm (accessed August 25, 2011).

Savage, Kirk. *Standing Soliders, Kneeling Slaves: Race, War and Monuments in Nineteenth-Century America.* Princeton, NJ: Princeton University, 1979.

Sherman, Ernest A. *Dedicating in Dixie.* Cedar Rapids, IA: Record Printing Co., 1907.

Shiloh Chapter of the United Daughters of the Confederacy Yearbook, 1998–2000. N.p., n.d.

Shiloh Commission Reports, Series I. Shiloh National Military Park, Shiloh, Tennessee.

Smith, Timothy B. "David W. Reed: The Father of Shiloh National Military Park." *Annals of Iowa* 62, no. 3 (Summer 2003): 333–59.

———. *The Golden Age of Battlefield Preservation: The Decade of the 1890s and the Establishment of America's First Five Military Parks.* Knoxville: University of Tennessee Press, 2008.

———. *This Great Battlefield of Shiloh: History, Memory and the Establishment of a Civil War National Military Park.* Knoxville: University of Tennessee Press, 2004.

Sword, Wiley. *Shiloh: Bloody April.* Dayton, OH: Morningside Bookshop, 1988.

Times-Picayune. "Dr. Lemonnier—Former Coroner Dies." January 15, 1928.

White, Mrs. Alexander. *Minutes of the 23rd Annual Convention of the UDC Held in Dallas, Texas.* Raleigh, NC: Edward and Broughton, 1917.

ABOUT THE AUTHOR

Dr. Stacy Reaves received her PhD from Oklahoma State University and is currently an adjunct professor of history and geography at Tulsa Community College. With a bachelor's degree in historic preservation, she has served as a museum director at Sand Springs Cultural and Historical Museum, museum curator at Sapulpa Historical Society and museum technician at Fort Sill Museum. She worked as a park interpreter and seasonal park ranger at the Shiloh National Military Park for five years. Dr. Reaves's writing has appeared in the *Chronicles of Oklahoma*, *North and South Magazine*, the *Journal of the West* and the *Journal of Military History*.